Communications in Computer and Information Science

2865

Series Editors

Gang Li, *School of Information Technology, Deakin University, Burwood, VIC, Australia*

Joaquim Filipe, *Polytechnic Institute of Setúbal, Setúbal, Portugal*

Zhiwei Xu, *Chinese Academy of Sciences, Beijing, China*

Rationale

The CCIS series is devoted to the publication of proceedings of computer science conferences. Its aim is to efficiently disseminate original research results in informatics in printed and electronic form. While the focus is on publication of peer-reviewed full papers presenting mature work, inclusion of reviewed short papers reporting on work in progress is welcome, too. Besides globally relevant meetings with internationally representative program committees guaranteeing a strict peer-reviewing and paper selection process, conferences run by societies or of high regional or national relevance are also considered for publication.

Topics

The topical scope of CCIS spans the entire spectrum of informatics ranging from foundational topics in the theory of computing to information and communications science and technology and a broad variety of interdisciplinary application fields.

Information for Volume Editors and Authors

Publication in CCIS is free of charge. No royalties are paid, however, we offer registered conference participants temporary free access to the online version of the conference proceedings on SpringerLink (http://link.springer.com) by means of an http referrer from the conference website and/or a number of complimentary printed copies, as specified in the official acceptance email of the event.

CCIS proceedings can be published in time for distribution at conferences or as postproceedings, and delivered in the form of printed books and/or electronically as USBs and/or e-content licenses for accessing proceedings at SpringerLink. Furthermore, CCIS proceedings are included in the CCIS electronic book series hosted in the SpringerLink digital library at http://link.springer.com/bookseries/7899. Conferences publishing in CCIS are allowed to use our online conference service (Meteor) for managing the whole proceedings lifecycle (from submission and reviewing to preparing for publication) free of charge.

Publication process

The language of publication is exclusively English. Authors publishing in CCIS have to sign the Springer CCIS copyright transfer form, however, they are free to use their material published in CCIS for substantially changed, more elaborate subsequent publications elsewhere. For the preparation of the camera-ready papers/files, authors have to strictly adhere to the Springer CCIS Authors' Instructions and are strongly encouraged to use the CCIS LaTeX style files or templates.

Abstracting/Indexing

CCIS is abstracted/indexed in DBLP, Google Scholar, EI-Compendex, Mathematical Reviews, SCImago, Scopus. CCIS volumes are also submitted for the inclusion in ISI Proceedings.

How to start

To start the evaluation of your proposal for inclusion in the CCIS series, please send an e-mail to ccis@springer.com

Kieran Woodward · Alicia Falcon-Caro ·
Richard Ramchurn · Steve Benford

Editors

Creative AI for Live Interactive Performances

First International Workshop
CLIP 2026, Singapore, January 26, 2026
Proceedings

 Springer

Editors
Kieran Woodward (iD)
University of Nottingham
Nottingham, UK

Alicia Falcon-Caro (iD)
University of Nottingham
Nottingham, UK

Richard Ramchurn
University of Nattingham
Nottingham, UK

Steve Benford
University of Nottingham
Nottingham, UK

ISSN 1865-0929   ISSN 1865-0937 (electronic)
Communications in Computer and Information Science
ISBN 978-3-032-16892-4   ISBN 978-3-032-16893-1 (eBook)
https://doi.org/10.1007/978-3-032-16893-1

© The Editor(s) (if applicable) and The Author(s), under exclusive license
to Springer Nature Switzerland AG 2026

This work is subject to copyright. All rights are solely and exclusively licensed by the Publisher, whether the whole or part of the material is concerned, specifically the rights of translation, reprinting, reuse of illustrations, recitation, broadcasting, reproduction on microfilms or in any other physical way, and transmission or information storage and retrieval, electronic adaptation, computer software, or by similar or dissimilar methodology now known or hereafter developed.
The use of general descriptive names, registered names, trademarks, service marks, etc. in this publication does not imply, even in the absence of a specific statement, that such names are exempt from the relevant protective laws and regulations and therefore free for general use.
The publisher, the authors and the editors are safe to assume that the advice and information in this book are believed to be true and accurate at the date of publication. Neither the publisher nor the authors or the editors give a warranty, expressed or implied, with respect to the material contained herein or for any errors or omissions that may have been made. The publisher remains neutral with regard to jurisdictional claims in published maps and institutional affiliations.

This Springer imprint is published by the registered company Springer Nature Switzerland AG
The registered company address is: Gewerbestrasse 11, 6330 Cham, Switzerland

If disposing of this product, please recycle the paper.

Preface

This volume contains the proceedings of the AAAI 2026 Workshop on Creative AI for Live Interactive Performances (CLIP), held on January 26, 2026, in Singapore, in conjunction with the 40th AAAI Conference on Artificial Intelligence.

The workshop brought together researchers exploring interactive creative AI systems that collaborate with humans across performing arts including music, visual arts and dance. Our central focus was designing AI systems that meaningfully participate in real-time creative workflows to enhance human performance. Unlike traditional generative AI producing finished outputs, interactive AI systems must respond dynamically to human input, adapt to context, and facilitate ongoing human-AI collaboration.

The workshop addressed unique technical and methodological challenges arising when AI systems interact with humans during creative processes, including how AI can respond to improvised and subjective performance in real-time, what interaction paradigms best support human-AI collaborative creativity, and how we evaluate systems where novelty and improvisation may be valued above correctness.

We received 15 submissions, all of which underwent a rigorous double-blind peer review process. Each paper was reviewed by at least three reviewers. Following the review process, 14 papers were accepted to attend the workshop and 8 were included in these proceedings. The accepted papers cover diverse topics, including creative AI for live interactive, interactive art through brain-computer interfaces, real-world applications of creative AI, music generation and evaluation methodologies for creative AI systems.

The workshop featured keynote presentations on AI for live performances and perspectives from performing artists, paper presentations, a poster session, structured group discussions on future research directions and ethics, and interactive demonstrations where participants showcased their work through physical demonstrations and video presentations.

We would like to thank all authors who submitted their work to the workshop, the Program Committee members and additional reviewers for their thorough reviews, our keynote speakers for sharing their expertise and insights, all participants for their contributions to the discussions and demonstrations, and the AAAI conference organisers for their support in hosting this workshop.

This work was supported by the Engineering and Physical Sciences Research Council (EPSRC) through the Turing AI World Leading Researcher Fellowship: Somabotics: Creatively Embodying Artificial Intelligence [grant number EP/Z534808/1].

December 2025

Kieran Woodward
Alicia Falcon-Caro
Richard Ramchurn
Steve Benford

Organization

Workshop Chair

Kieran Woodward — School of Computer Science, University of
Nottingham, UK

Program Committee Chairs

Alicia Falcon-Caro — School of Medicine, University of Nottingham,
UK

Richard Ramchurn — School of Computer Science, University of
Nottingham, UK

Steve Benford — School of Computer Science, University of
Nottingham, UK

Additional Reviewers

Alan Chamberlain
Maria Elena Giannaccini
Matthew Harris
Zane Hartley
Thomas Johnson
John Kiran

Ayse Kucukyilmaz
Bradley Patrick
Dominic Price
Teena Rai
Caroline Zheng

Contents

Overview

Creative AI for Live Interactive Performances: Foundations, Challenges, and Future Directions

Kieran Woodward[1]([✉]) (iD), Alicia Falcon-Caro[2], Richard Ramchurn[1], and Steve Benford[1]

[1] School of Computer Science, University of Nottingham, Nottingham, UK
{kieran.woodward1,richard.ramchurn,steve.benford}@nottingham.ac.uk
[2] School of Medicine, University of Nottingham, Nottingham, UK
alicia.falconcaro@nottingham.ac.uk

Abstract. Creative AI research has mostly focused on generating text, images and videos, with limited exploration of live interactive performances. This work examines the challenges and opportunities that emerge when AI systems must operate in real-time, responding dynamically to human collaborators through embodied interaction. Unlike offline generative systems, real-time AI must meet temporal constraints that vary by modality, integrate multi-modal sensing and navigate subjective criteria where novelty may be valued over consistency. The paper introduces Somabotics as an approach that utilises artistic practice to design embodied AI experiences where robots engage human meaning-making through bodily interaction, employing methodologies including performance-led research in the wild and soma design. Emerging research directions include personalisation and long-term adaptation, enabling sustained creative partnerships, cross-modal translation and collective creativity. Advancing this field requires not only technical innovation but also diverse datasets capturing artistic performance, evaluation frameworks appropriate for subjective creative domains and inter-disciplinary collaboration between machine learning, human-computer interaction researchers and artists. Creative performance offers unique contexts for exploring how AI systems can meaningfully participate in activities where real-time collaboration, embodied experience and aesthetic quality matter.

Keywords: Creative AI · Generative AI · Live Interactive Performance · Real-Time · Somabotics · Robotics · Multi-Modal

1 Introduction

In recent years there has been ever increasing focus on generative AI and its role in creativity. However, the vast majority of this work focuses on text, images and videos [70], there is little research into how creative AI can play a role in live interactive performances. While generative AI systems like Large Language

© The Author(s), under exclusive license to Springer Nature Switzerland AG 2026

K. Woodward et al. (Eds.): CLIP 2026, CCIS 2865, pp. 3–21, 2026.
https://doi.org/10.1007/978-3-032-16893-1_1

Models (LLM) and image generators have demonstrated remarkable capabilities in producing creative work, live performance presents fundamentally different challenges and opportunities. Live performances unfold in real-time with human collaborators who improvise, adapt and respond to context.

There has been an increase in creative AI research from disembodied systems toward physical, embodied platforms [69]. This turn to embodiment reflects growing recognition that many forms of creative expression, particularly in performance are fundamentally live activities that unfold through people moving in space and sharing presence with audiences.

Embodiment is highly important for live performance in several ways, physicality enables forms of expression and communication that traditional AI cannot express. Co-presence creates unique temporal and social dynamics. For example, when a dancer shares space with robots, both the performer and audience are exploring risk, intimacy and possibilities that remain inaccessible in disembodied AI. Live performance unfolds over time, with all participants experiencing the same unrepeatable moment and this shared experience enables forms of improvisation and responsiveness that differ from asynchronous interaction with generated content.

The technical requirements of live interactive performance push beyond current generative AI paradigms. Latency constraints vary dramatically by modality. For example, musical interaction may require responses within milliseconds, while dance might afford slightly more flexibility yet still demand fluid, naturalistic timing. Beyond technical challenges, interactive AI raises methodological questions, such as; How do we design AI systems in collaboration with artists who may value aesthetic qualities rather than considering technical capabilities? How do we evaluate systems where *errors* might be creatively valuable, and where subjective experience matters as much as objective metrics? Traditional machine learning evaluation frameworks which focus on accuracy and reproducibility often misalign with artistic values that prioritise novelty, creativity and variation.

The embodied, practice-led nature of creative AI research requires methodologies that can accommodate open-ended exploration, subjective evaluation, and emerging insights. Research through design is a constructive, practice-led approach where knowledge emerges from creating and reflecting on portfolios [8]. Rather than beginning with hypotheses tested through controlled experiments, research through design researchers create systems or experiences, deploy them and then reflect on what these creations reveal about design, user experiences or theoretical concepts. For embodied creative AI, research through design offers several advantages, it accommodates the exploratory, iterative nature of both artistic practice and technical development, and it recognises that creating working systems in real-world environments generates insights impossible to anticipate through purely theoretical analysis.

Artistic practice plays an essential role in advancing embodied creative AI, not merely as an application for existing techniques but as a source of novel research, design insights and evaluation frameworks. Artists bring unique forms of expertise including aesthetic judgement, acceptance for ambiguity, experience navigating open-ended creative processes and the ability to engage audiences with complex ideas through experiential means. When artists and researchers collaborate, technical systems develop in response to creative needs whilst artistic outcomes benefit from technical capabilities that expand expressive possibilities.

This paper examines the foundations, challenges and future directions for creative AI in live interactive performance. Section 2 introduces Somabotics as a methodology that addresses these challenges through artistic practice; Sect. 3 discusses the technical foundations and challenges that distinguish real-time performance from offline generation; Sect. 4 outlines emerging research opportunities in personalisation, cross-modal translation, and collective creativity, and Sect. 5 concludes.

2   Somabotics

Somabotics aims to utilise artistic practice to design embodied AI experiences where robots help explore human meaning-making through bodily engagement. The approach helps addresses the challenges that limit AI's potential in creative performance contexts.

The experience challenge explores how AI needs to engage humans in meaningful experiences. Somabotics introduces ambiguities throughout the design process to enable interpretation [30]. While this is an alternative approach to traditional AI, this approach is similar to that used in Human-Computer Interaction (HCI), humanities and art. The embodiment challenge recognises that people make meaning through their bodies as well as their minds. For AI to engage human meaning-making in live interactive performance, it must engage people through their bodies, which requires AI itself to be embodied. Robots enable AI to have physical embodiment with sensing and actuation in collaboration with people. Finally, the meaningful AI challenge explores how humans make sense of AI in creative practice as art is uniquely positioned to engage audiences with complex challenges through experiential means.

Somabotics employs two methodologies relevant to creative real-time AI. Performance-led research in the wild [8] involves collaboration with artists to create and study interactive artworks. Artists maintain creative control whilst researchers support technical development and study audience experience. Soma design places bodily experience at the centre of technology design [38,43], therefore performers, designers and researchers can explore robotics and AI through movement and touch.

Deployed artworks include Embrace Angels [53], exploring human-robot embraces using dual-arm robots, Different Bodies - Dancing with Robots [7] exploring creative motion generation, Pamper Factory examining trust of robots grooming guided by AI and Intelligent Instruments [6] enabling real-time folk music improvisation. These projects demonstrate how artistic practice drives technical innovation. While Somabotics provides a framework for embodied creative AI, realising these artistic visions in live performance contexts highlights numerous technical challenges that must be addressed across real-time systems, sensing, generation and interaction design.

3 Technical Foundations, Platforms and Challenges of Live Interactive AI

3.1 Real-Time Deployment Constraints and Latency

Live interactive performance imposes temporal constraints that differentiate it from offline generative AI applications [98]. The latency requirements vary dramatically by modality and determine which architectures and deployment strategies remain viable [9]. These constraints immediately rule out many recent generative deep learning approaches. Large language models with billions of parameters introduce latencies measured in seconds when generating tokens autoregressively [48]. Similarly, diffusion models for image and video generation can require hundreds of denoising steps, making real-time deployment challenging even with significant computational resources [14]. The technical challenge therefore becomes identifying the minimal model complexity sufficient for expressive generation whilst meeting temporal constraints.

Several strategies address these constraints. Distillation techniques train smaller student networks to approximate the behaviour of larger teacher models, trading some representational capacity for reduced inference time. Knowledge distillation has proven particularly effective for transferring learned patterns from large offline models to compact real-time systems [35]. Progressive inference architectures generate coarse outputs quickly and refine them iteratively, allowing systems to respond immediately whilst improving quality over subsequent timesteps [47]. This approach proves valuable in contexts where some response latency is acceptable but complete absence of feedback would disrupt interaction flow.

Edge computing versus cloud processing represents another trade-off. Cloud deployment provides access to substantial computational resources including GPUs that enable more complex models, but introduces network latency that may be unacceptable for live applications [83]. Edge deployment on local hardware ensures minimal latency but constrains model complexity to what embedded processors can execute in real-time [31,32,51].

Model architecture choices have a direct impact on latency characteristics. Recurrent neural networks including Long Short-Term Memory (LSTM) networks and Gated Recurrent Units (GRU) process sequences incrementally, making them naturally suited to streaming data where each timestep's output depends only on current input and hidden state [72]. Transformer architectures, whilst powerful for capturing long-range dependencies, traditionally require full sequence context and therefore struggle with real-time processing [28,29,63,73]. However, recent developments including streaming transformers [17] attempt to address this limitation by maintaining compact state representations that can be updated incrementally without reprocessing entire histories.

3.2 Multi-modal Sensing and Understanding

Live performance typically involves multiple sensory modalities such as haptics, vision and audio. The technical challenge of sensor fusion involves integrating these modalities into unified representations. Different sensors operate at different sampling rates, exhibit different noise characteristics, require different preprocessing and have different latencies [1,52]. Simply concatenating features from different modalities into high-dimensional vectors is often not ideal. Recent approaches employ learned multi-modal fusion where neural networks project different input modalities into shared embedding spaces [76]. Attention mechanisms enable models to dynamically weight different modalities based on context, for example attending to visual information during initial phases of approach and then attending to haptic data once physical contact is established [36,96].

Temporal alignment poses additional challenges. Visual tracking, audio analysis and force sensing may operate at different rates and exhibit different processing delays therefore accurate temporal synchronisation requires careful system design. Kalman filtering and particle filtering offer probabilistic frameworks for fusing measurements with different uncertainties and update rates [18], although deep learning approaches including recurrent neural networks and temporal convolutional networks increasingly handle alignment through learned representations.

3.3 Real-Time Model Generation

Generation in real-time performance contexts requires models that produce contextually appropriate, temporally coherent outputs while remaining responsive to real-time input. Conditioned generation [21] provides one framework where models learn mappings from context vectors to output distributions. Variational autoencoders (VAE) [50] learn latent representations of training data and enable generation by sampling from learned distributions conditioned on context. Generative adversarial networks (GAN) [34] train generators to produce samples indistinguishable from training data according to learned discriminators. Whilst GANs have proven effective for image generation, their application to temporal sequences including music and motion remains more challenging due to mode collapse and training instability [12].

Transformer architectures have emerged as powerful sequence models capable of capturing long-range dependencies through self-attention mechanisms [80]. For musical generation, models including Music Transformer [40] and MuseNet [71] demonstrate impressive capability for generating coherent multi-bar compositions. However, these models typically train on representations such as MIDI and operate autoregressively, predicting one token at a time conditioned on all previous tokens. This autoregressive generation introduces latency that may be unacceptable for real-time interaction. Recent work explores non-autoregressive generation [100] that trade some output quality for reduced latency.

For motion generation, several approaches have proven effective. Recurrent networks including LSTMs can generate human motion by predicting joint angles or positions at each timestep conditioned on previous poses [97]. Graph convolutional networks leverage the skeletal structure of human bodies, treating joints as nodes and bones as edges in a graph, enabling models to learn spatially structured representations [26,93]. Motion in context typically requires conditioning not only on previous poses but also on goals, environment constraints, and interaction partners. Inverse reinforcement learning [5] and imitation learning from demonstration [41] offer frameworks for learning policies that generate motion satisfying complex implicit objectives.

Many approaches exist that could be beneficial in live creative AI. Meta-learning trains models that can quickly adapt to new tasks with minimal fine-tuning data [39] which can enable new artistic concepts to be quickly explored. Few-shot learning [82] enables personalisation from small numbers of examples, which proves essential in artistic contexts where capturing extensive training data from individual performers may be impractical. Similarly, transfer learning [99] leverages models pre-trained on large general datasets and fine-tunes them on smaller domain-specific datasets, enabling systems to benefit from broad patterns whilst specialising to particular artistic contexts [89]. Reinforcement Learning (RL) [61] offers frameworks for systems that learn through interaction rather than supervised imitation. By defining reward functions capturing desired performance qualities, RL enables exploration of novel behaviours not present in training data. However, defining appropriate reward functions for creative tasks remains challenging, as desirable qualities including expressiveness, novelty, and aesthetic coherence are not simple to quantify. Inverse reinforcement learning [5] attempts to infer reward functions from expert demonstrations, learning implicit objectives that generate observed behaviour. These learning paradigms highlight many opportunities for creative applications but also highlight a fundamental challenge in the need to balance learning from existing artistic practices while simultaneously enabling novelty and creative exploration.

3.4   Interaction Paradigms

The design space for human-AI interaction in performance spans across multiple dimensions. At one end, AI systems can be controlled by performers through commands or continuous parameters. This preserves human control but may limit the sense of collaboration. At the other end, fully autonomous AI systems make the creative decisions, potentially creating interesting surprises but risking conflicts with performer intentions [37,60]. Most successful systems balance this control, where performers influence the AI whilst the AI exercises autonomy within predefined constraints [6].

Turn-taking versus continuous interaction represents another option. Turn-taking systems, common in conversational interfaces [15] and some music applications alternate between human and AI contributions [85]. This simplifies coordination but may feel unnatural in contexts where seamless integration is preferred. Continuous interaction, where human and AI contributions occur simultaneously and influence each other in real-time better captures the natural nature of creative live performances but requires careful design to avoid conflicts.

Mixed initiative interaction attempts to balance these considerations by enabling both human and AI to initiate actions and control interaction [22,56]. This requires systems capable of recognising when human performers are leading versus following and when they are open to AI compared to focused on their own ideas. Implementing mixed-initiative systems requires addressing multiple challenges including determining what elements of control to share, when to transfer control and how to coordinate the handoff [46].

3.5 Robotics and Creative AI

Robots have the potential to serve multiple roles in creative performance including as instruments controlled by performers, as autonomous co-performers collaborating with humans and as physical embodiments of AI systems [27]. Each role imposes different technical requirements and design considerations.

Expressive motion generation for robots differs fundamentally from functional manipulation. Industrial robot control focuses on accuracy, repeatability and efficiency in achieving well-defined tasks [42]. Creative motion prioritises aesthetic qualities including rhythm, dynamics, spatial patterns and emotional expressiveness [20]. These metrics are not easily quantified and often require learning from demonstration [4,65] or exploration through reinforcement learning [44,62]. Motion capture of performers provides training data although transferring human motion to robots with different kinematics requires algorithms that preserve essential qualities whilst considering mechanical feasibility. Cross-modal style transfer approaches can adapt existing robot trajectories to new movement styles using few-shot learning from video demonstrations, requiring only 3–6 examples to transfer characteristics such as rhythm and acceleration patterns from human dancers to robot motion whilst maintaining trajectory integrity [87].

Robots have been deployed in diverse creative contexts that emphasise collaboration, social interaction and artistic expression. Dance represents a particularly rich domain where robots serve as performers, partners or interactive elements within choreography. Human-robot artistic collaboration has been explored through systems where robots autonomously execute dance movements whilst AI mediates parameter adaptation, such as a Pepper robot performing classical ballet patterns that dynamically adjust to match the artistic moods expressed by a jazz pianist [78]. Physical touch and intimate interaction have emerged as meaningful modes of autonomous creative expression, with robots designed to deliver hugs that balance physical comfort with technical capabilities [10]. Theatrical contexts have explored robots as co-performers requiring systems that coordinate with human actors while also responding to improvisation [58]. Multi-robot systems create possibilities for collective choreography where individual agents coordinate to produce emergent patterns, enabling artistic expressions that explore swarm behaviour, synchronisation and distributed agency [19]. These creative applications share common technical requirements including real-time responsiveness, expressive movement generation and safe human proximity, while also introducing domain-specific challenges around artistic intent, audience experience and aesthetic quality.

Furthermore, safety considerations in performance contexts differ from industrial settings. Performers may deliberately seek close physical contact and even collisions that would be unacceptable in industrial environments. However, the presence of audiences, performance spaces and unpredictable performer behaviour require careful consideration. Force limiting through compliant mechanisms and torque sensing enables robots to detect unexpected contacts and respond appropriately [2,57,75]. Redundant safety systems including emergency stops and physical barriers provide an extra layer of safety but creative exploration may require accepting additional risks that would be eliminated in purely functional applications.

3.6 Brain-Computer Interfaces and Creative Expression

Brain-Computer Interfaces (BCI) offer possibilities for creative performance by enabling systems to respond to cognitive and emotional states inferred from brain activity. Electroencephalography (EEG) represents the most practical BCI modality for performance given its non-invasiveness and portability although it is susceptible to artefacts from movement and muscle activity [16].

BCI systems for creativity typically operate in four methods of control selective control, passive control, direct control and collaborative control [81]. Direct control BCIs enable performers to trigger actions through voluntary mental activity including motor imagery, attention shifts or learned mental strategies. This requires training both the performer to produce reliable signals and the system to decode intended commands from noisy neural data. The cognitive load of maintaining control while also engaging in creative performance presents challenges as sustained attention may interfere with spontaneous artistic practice [66].

Passive monitoring BCIs instead track cognitive and emotional states without requiring direct control. Systems could detect attention levels, emotional valence and arousal or cognitive workload [94]. This information can alter AI behaviour for example increasing system autonomy when performer attention is focused elsewhere or adapting difficulty based on cognitive load. However, inferring subjective states from physiological signals [59] remains challenging due to individual differences and performance contexts [25].

Music applications of BCI have demonstrated both direct control and passive monitoring approaches. Direct control systems enable performers to trigger musical events through motor imagery or attention [81]. The Encephalophone [23] allows performers to control pitch by focusing attention on specific visual stimuli, enabling musical expression for individuals with severe motor disabilities [24]. Passive monitoring approaches use detected emotional states to influence generative music systems, creating compositions that reflect performer mental state [33,67]. Visual art applications employ BCI for generative drawing and painting. Systems translate neural signals including attention and emotional arousal into brush strokes, colours or visual patterns [11,77]. Artistic applications of BCI for live performance have explored multi-modal feedback from brain activity during intimate social interaction. EEG KISS involved participants kissing whilst wearing EEG headsets, with their brain activity visualised through floor projections and translated into real-time soundscapes for surrounding spectators [54]. In theatrical contexts, researchers have explored using EEG headsets to enable viewers to generate personalised edits of films through subconscious attention-based control, where drops in measured attention trigger cuts between parallel narrative threads [64].

Signal processing for BCI in performance contexts must balance competing demands, as artefact filtering may remove useful movement-related signals. Moreover, the cognitive load required to maintain BCI control can interfere with creative flow and spontaneous artistic expression. These challenges highlight the need for interaction paradigms that support the embodied nature of live performance.

3.7 Evaluating Creative AI

Evaluating creative AI systems for live performance presents challenges because traditional machine learning metrics often misalign with artistic values and performance quality. Accuracy, precision, and recall measure how well systems match reference data but creative performance may value novelty and divergence from training examples. Mean squared error and other regression metrics assume that minimising deviation from targets is desirable but creative practice often seeks surprise.

Qualitative evaluation methods offer complementary approaches [8]. Semi-structured interviews with performers explore subjective experience including feelings of agency, creative flow and sense of partnership with AI systems. These interviews can reveal interaction qualities that quantitative metrics miss such as whether systems feel responsive, predictable, surprising or inspiring.

Observational studies can also document how performers interact with systems such what strategies they develop, where errors occur and how they recover from technical failures. Audience experience represents another evaluation option, as the aim of live performances is to engage the audience where post-performance questionnaires and interviews can assess audience engagement, emotional response and perception of AI. However, audience feedback reflects post-performance opinions rather than in-the-moment experience. Physiological measures including heart rate variability, electrodermal activity and facial expression analysis offer continuous indicators of audience arousal and affect [86,88], although interpreting these signals requires care given individual differences and context effects [90].

On the other hand, performers, audiences, critics, and researchers may value different qualities and assess success using different criteria. Performers may prioritise artistic innovation, audiences may value emotional engagement and researchers may focus on technical novelty and generalisability. Therefore, comprehensive evaluation requires gathering and integrating these multiple perspectives rather than focusing on a single criteria.

4   Emerging Research Opportunities

The field of creative AI for live interactive performance remains in its early stages, with numerous challenges and opportunities for future research. This section identifies several promising directions across technical and performance domains, highlighting both immediate research needs and longer-term goals.

4.1   Personalisation and Long-Term Adaptation

Current creative AI systems typically operate in relatively short timescales, responding to immediate context within individual performances. However, creative collaborations between humans and AI systems require longer-term adaptation where systems learn individual performer styles, preferences and creative tendencies over extended periods. This presents several technical challenges beyond standard transfer learning or few-shot learning approaches.

Continual learning frameworks [84] enable systems to learn knowledge from ongoing experience without catastrophic forgetting of previously learned patterns [68]. However, creative partnerships also require systems to introduce novelty rather than merely imitating learned patterns. The technical challenge therefore becomes developing models that balance consistency with novelty.

Affective computing techniques that track emotional valence and arousal over time could enable systems to learn which behaviours elicit positive responses and which create frustration or disengagement. However, this raises concerns about systems optimising for immediate pleasure rather than longer-term creative development. Meta-learning approaches that learn how to adapt to new performers quickly might enable systems to personalise efficiently even with limited interaction history. Few-shot imitation learning and meta-learning offer promising starting points, although their application to creative domains requires further development.

Overall, consistency enables performers to develop reliable interaction strategies and build intuition about system behaviour, however continuous evolution might keep interactions novel and unique. Hybrid approaches where systems maintain core characteristics whilst varying features offer potential compromise. Understanding performer preferences regarding consistency and novelty requires further investigation across different artistic domains and individual differences.

4.2   Cross-Modal Translation

Many compelling creative applications involve translating between artistic modalities, for example generating movement from music, producing visual imagery from sound or creating haptic patterns from visual input.

Recent approaches to cross-modal generation typically employ encoder-decoder architectures where encoders map input modalities to shared latent representations and decoders generate output modalities from these representations [3]. Variational autoencoders, generative adversarial networks and diffusion models provide frameworks for learning these mappings from paired training data.

However, obtaining large datasets of aligned multi-modal artistic data presents practical challenges.

Self-supervised learning [45,74] and contrastive learning [49,79] offer potential approaches for learning cross-modal representations without requiring explicit paired data. By learning representations where temporally co-occurring signals from different modalities map to similar latent codes, systems might discover implicit relationships. However, temporal co-occurrence does not guarantee meaningful relationship. Alternatively, attention mechanisms [80] and cross-modal transformers [92] enable models to learn which aspects of one modality should influence which aspects of another. Learning these correspondences requires architectures that can discover and apply modality-specific mappings rather than assuming uniform translation rules.

4.3   Collective and Distributed Creativity

Most research on creative AI focuses on interaction between individual humans and AI systems. However, live performances often involve multiple performers who coordinate and respond to each other dynamically. Extending creative AI to these contexts introduces technical challenges around multi-agent coordination, emergent behaviour and distributed decision-making.

Multi-agent reinforcement learning [13] provides frameworks for training systems that coordinate without centralised control. Each agent learns based on local observations and rewards, with coordination emerging from repeated interaction. However, creative performance differs from typical multi-agent domains like games or robotics tasks because the notion of optimal behaviour remains context-dependent. Therefore, the reward function for creative applications presents challenges as well as the challenge of determining which agents' actions contributed to the desirable outputs.

Graph neural networks [91] offer promising architectures for modelling ensembles where relationships between performers matter. Treating performers as nodes and their relationships as edges, graph networks can learn representations that capture ensemble structure. Attention mechanisms enable models to weight different relationships dynamically, for example focusing on leader-follower interaction in some contexts whilst attending to paired interaction in others. However, performance relationships are often dynamic rather than forming fixed graphs, requiring architectures that can discover and adapt to changing interaction patterns.

Networked and distributed performances where participants interact from different physical locations introduce additional technical requirements around latency and bandwidth management. Distributed training [55] and federated learning [95] approaches might enable systems to learn from multiple interactions without requiring centralised data collection, preserving privacy whilst benefiting from diverse data.

5   Conclusion

Creative AI for live interactive performance represents a unique and interesting domain that challenges many underlying assumptions of modern AI research. Unlike offline generative systems that produce finished artefacts, creative interactive AI must operate in real-time, responding dynamically to human collaborators whilst maintaining temporal coherence and aesthetic quality across extended interactions. Furthermore unlike disembodied systems, embodied performance AI engages through movement, touch and co-presence and must allow for subjective judgements where novelty may be valued over consistency and reliability.

These distinctive characteristics require technical innovations across low-latency architectures that meet strict temporal constraints across multiple modalities, multi-modal fusion approaches that integrate multiple sensor streams into coherent representations and interaction techniques that support creative collaboration rather than just generation. They also require methodological innovations including practice-led research approaches that position artistic exploration as knowledge generation and evaluation approaches that accommodate subjective experience alongside quantitative metrics.

This field faces numerous challenges and opportunities. Personalisation and long-term adaptation could enable systems that develop creative relationships with individual performers, learning styles and preferences whilst maintaining the capability to generate novel outputs. Cross-modal translation might bridge artistic domains, however advancing this research requires not just new algorithms but also diverse datasets capturing artistic performance and evaluation frameworks appropriate for subjective creative domains.

Furthermore, creative AI for live interactive performance requires interdisciplinary collaboration. Machine learning researchers bring expertise in architectures, training strategies, and optimisation but may lack understanding of aesthetic judgement, performance conventions and bodily experience. Artists possess knowledge about expressiveness, timing and audience engagement but may struggle with technical constraints and computational thinking.

As AI capabilities continue advancing, creative performance becomes increasingly important for understanding how AI can meaningfully participate in open-ended activities. The challenges of designing AI systems that collaborate rather than purely assist and establishing appropriate forms of agency in real-time contexts are highlighted in live interactive systems with creative practice offering invaluable contexts for exploring these challenges.

Acknowledgments. This work was supported by the Engineering and Physical Sciences Research Council (EPSRC) through the Turing AI World Leading Researcher Fellowship: Somabotics: Creatively Embodying Artificial Intelligence [grant number EP/Z534808/1].

References

1. Abate, F., Huang, V.K., Monte, G., Paciello, V., Pietrosanto, A.: A comparison between sensor signal preprocessing techniques. IEEE Sens. J. **15**, 2479–2487 (2015). https://doi.org/10.1109/JSEN.2014.2341742
2. Aivaliotis, P., Aivaliotis, S., Gkournelos, C., Kokkalis, K., Michalos, G., Makris, S.: Power and force limiting on industrial robots for human-robot collaboration. Robot. Comput.-Integr. Manufact. **59**, 346–360 (2019). https://doi.org/10.1016/J.RCIM.2019.05.001
3. Akbari, H., et al.: Vatt: transformers for multimodal self-supervised learning from raw video, audio and text. Adv. Neural Inf. Process. Syst. **34**, 24206–24221 (2021)
4. Argall, B.D., Chernova, S., Veloso, M., Browning, B.: A survey of robot learning from demonstration. Robot. Auton. Syst. **57**, 469–483 (2009). https://doi.org/10.1016/J.ROBOT.2008.10.024
5. Arora, S., Doshi, P.: A survey of inverse reinforcement learning: challenges, methods and progress. Artif. Intell. **297**, 103500 (2021). https://doi.org/10.1016/J.ARTINT.2021.103500
6. Benford, S., Amerotti, M., Sturm, B.L., Avila, J.M.: Negotiating autonomy and trust when performing with an ai musician. In: ACM International Conference Proceeding Series (2024). https://doi.org/10.1145/3686038.3686040/SUPPL_FILE/GLITCH2.MOV
7. Benford, S., et al.: How artists improvise and provoke robotics, pp. 66–77 (2025). https://doi.org/10.1007/978-981-96-3525-2_6
8. Benford, S., et al.: Performance-led research in the wild. ACM Trans. Comput.-Hum. Interact. (TOCHI) **20** (2013). https://doi.org/10.1145/2491500.2491502
9. Bieniek, J., Rahouti, M., Verma, D.C.: Generative ai in multimodal user interfaces: trends, challenges, and cross-platform adaptability (2024). https://arxiv.org/abs/2411.10234v1
10. Block, A.E., Seifi, H., Hilliges, O., Gassert, R., Kuchenbecker, K.J.: In the arms of a robot: designing autonomous hugging robots with intra-hug gestures. ACM Trans. Hum.-Robot Interact. **12** (2023). https://doi.org/10.1145/3526110/ASSET/38619F13-168A-48F5-9110-99F4505801A0/ASSETS/IMAGES/LARGE/THRI-2021-0001-F22.JPG. https://dl.acm.org/doi/10.1145/3526110
11. Botrel, L., Holz, E.M., Kübler, A.: Brain painting v2: evaluation of p300-based brain-computer interface for creative expression by an end-user following the user-centered design. Brain-Comput. Interfaces **2**, 135–149 (2015). https://doi.org/10.1080/2326263X.2015.1100038
12. Brophy, E., Wang, Z., She, Q., Ward, T.: Generative adversarial networks in time series: a systematic literature review. ACM Comput. Surv. **55** (2023). https://doi.org/10.1145/3559540/ASSET/4230F9BD-47FD-4192-90E6-FA0A299FB02A/ASSETS/IMAGES/LARGE/CSUR-2021-0379-F14.JPG. https://dl.acm.org/doi/10.1145/3559540
13. Buşoniu, L., Babuška, R., Schutter, B.D.: Multi-agent reinforcement learning: an overview. Studies in Computational Intelligence, vol. 310, pp. 183–221 (2010). https://doi.org/10.1007/978-3-642-14435-6_7
14. Cao, H., et al.: A survey on generative diffusion models. IEEE Trans. Knowl. Data Eng. **36**, 2814–2830 (2024). https://doi.org/10.1109/TKDE.2024.3361474
15. Cassell, J.: Embodied conversational agents: representation and intelligence in user interfaces. AI Mag. **22**, 67 (2001). https://doi.org/10.1609/AIMAG.V22I4.1593

16. Lan Chen, L., Zhang, A., Guang Lou, X.: Cross-subject driver status detection from physiological signals based on hybrid feature selection and transfer learning. Expert Syst. Appl. (2019). https://doi.org/10.1016/j.eswa.2019.02.005
17. Chen, X., Wu, Y., Wang, Z., Liu, S., Li, J.: Developing real-time streaming transformer transducer for speech recognition on large-scale dataset. In: ICASSP, IEEE International Conference on Acoustics, Speech and Signal Processing - Proceedings 2021-June, pp. 5904–5908 (2021). https://doi.org/10.1109/ICASSP39728.2021.9413535
18. Chen, Z.: Bayesian filtering: from Kalman filters to particle filters, and beyond. Statistics (2003)
19. Cuan, C., et al.: Interactive multi-robot flocking with gesture responsiveness and musical accompaniment. ACM Trans. Human-Robot Interact. (2025). https://doi.org/10.1145/3762675. https://dl.acm.org/doi/10.1145/3762675
20. Cubero, C.G., Pekarik, M., Rizzo, V., Jochum, E.: The robot is present: creative approaches for artistic expression with robots. Front. Robot. AI **8**, 662249 (2021). https://doi.org/10.3389/FROBT.2021.662249/BIBTEX. www.frontiersin.org
21. Den, A.V., et al.: Conditional image generation with pixelcnn decoders. Adv. Neural Inf. Process. Syst. **29** (2016)
22. Deterding, S., et al.: Mixed-initiative creative interfaces. In: Conference on Human Factors in Computing Systems - Proceedings Part F127655, pp. 628–635 (2017). https://doi.org/10.1145/3027063.3027072
23. Deuel, T.A., Pampin, J., Sundstrom, J., Darvas, F.: The encephalophone: a novel musical biofeedback device using conscious control of electroencephalogram (EEG). Front. Hum. Neurosci. **11**, 205372 (2017). https://doi.org/10.3389/FNHUM.2017.00213/BIBTEX
24. Deuel, T.A., Wenlock, J., McGovern, A., Rosenthal, J., Pampin, J.: Musical auditory feedback BCI: clinical pilot study of the encephalophone. Front. Hum. Neurosci. **19**, 1592640 (2025). https://doi.org/10.3389/FNHUM.2025.1592640/BIBTEX
25. Dietrich, A., Kanso, R.: A review of EEG, ERP, and neuroimaging studies of creativity and insight. Psychol. Bull. **136**, 822–848 (2010). https://doi.org/10.1037/A0019749
26. Ferreira, J.P., et al.: Learning to dance: a graph convolutional adversarial network to generate realistic dance motions from audio. Comput. Graph. **94**, 11–21 (2021). https://doi.org/10.1016/J.CAG.2020.09.009
27. Formosa, P.: Robot autonomy vs. human autonomy: social robots, artificial intelligence (AI), and the nature of autonomy. Minds Mach. **31**, 595–616 (2021). https://doi.org/10.1007/S11023-021-09579-2/METRICS
28. Fournier, Q., Caron, G.M., Aloise, D.: A practical survey on faster and lighter transformers. ACM Comput. Surv. **55** (2024). https://doi.org/10.1145/3586074/ASSET/6847FB60-595A-4166-BF4E-2291E1F0CB0F/ASSETS/IMAGES/LARGE/CSUR-2022-0071-F18.JPG
29. Fu, Y.: Challenges in deploying long-context transformers: a theoretical peak performance analysis (2024). https://arxiv.org/abs/2405.08944v1
30. Gaver, W.W., Beaver, J., Benford, S.: Ambiguity as a resource for design. In: Conference on Human Factors in Computing Systems - Proceedings, pp. 233–240 (2003). https://doi.org/10.1145/642611.642653. https://dl.acm.org/doi/10.1145/642611.642653
31. Gibbs, M., Woodward, K., Kanjo, E.: Combining multiple tinyml models for multimodal context-aware stress recognition on constrained microcontrollers. IEEE Micro 1–9 (2023). https://doi.org/10.1109/MM.2023.3329218

32. Giorgetti, G., Pau, D.P.: Transitioning from tinyml to edge genai: a review. Big Data Cogn. Comput. **9**, 61 (2025). https://doi.org/10.3390/BDCC9030061
33. Glassman, H., Dwyer, D., John, N., Laesker, D., So, M.: Affective brain-computer music interface in emotion regulation and neurofeedback: a research protocol. Undergraduate Res. Nat. Clin. Sci. Technol. J. **6**, 1–9 (2022). https://doi.org/10.26685/URNCST.345
34. Goodfellow, I., et al.: Generative adversarial networks. Commun. ACM **63**, 139–144 (2020). https://doi.org/10.1145/3422622
35. Gou, J., Yu, B., Maybank, S.J., Tao, D.: Knowledge distillation: a survey. Int. J. Comput. Vision **129**, 1789–1819 (2021). https://doi.org/10.1007/S11263-021-01453-Z/TABLES/6
36. Han, X., et al.: Multimodal fusion and vision–language models: a survey for robot vision. Inf. Fusion **126**, 103652 (2026). https://doi.org/10.1016/J.INFFUS.2025.103652
37. He, H., Gray, J., Cangelosi, A., Meng, Q., McGinnity, T.M., Mehnen, J.: The challenges and opportunities of human-centered ai for trustworthy robots and autonomous systems. IEEE Trans. Cogn. Dev. Syst. **14**, 1398–1412 (2022). https://doi.org/10.1109/TCDS.2021.3132282
38. Hook, K.: Designing with the body: somaesthetic interaction design. MIT Press (2018)
39. Hospedales, T., Antoniou, A., Micaelli, P., Storkey, A.: Meta-learning in neural networks: a survey. IEEE Trans. Pattern Anal. Mach. Intell. **44**, 5149–5169 (2022). https://doi.org/10.1109/TPAMI.2021.3079209
40. Huang, J., Lian, Z., Li, Y., Niu, M., Tao, J., Yang, M.: Deep learning for continuous multiple time series annotations. In: AVEC 2018 - Proceedings of the 2018 Audio/Visual Emotion Challenge and Workshop, co-located with MM 2018, pp. 99–105. Association for Computing Machinery, Inc (2018). https://doi.org/10.1145/3266302.3266305
41. Hussein, A., Gaber, M.M., Elyan, E., Jayne, C.: Imitation learning: a survey of learning methods. ACM Comput. Surv. (CSUR) **50** (2017). https://doi.org/10.1145/3054912
42. Hägele, M., Nilsson, K., Pires, J.N., Bischoff, R.: Industrial robotics. In: Siciliano, B., Khatib, O. (eds.) Springer Handbook of Robotics, pp. 1385–1422. Springer, Cham (2016). https://doi.org/10.1007/978-3-319-32552-1_54
43. Höök, K., Jonsson, M.P., Ståhl, A., Mercurio, J.: Somaesthetic appreciation design. In: Conference on Human Factors in Computing Systems - Proceedings (2016). https://doi.org/10.1145/2858036.2858583
44. Ibarz, J., Tan, J., Finn, C., Kalakrishnan, M., Pastor, P., Levine, S.: How to train your robot with deep reinforcement learning: lessons we have learned. Int. J. Robot. Res. **40**, 698–721 (2021). https://doi.org/10.1177/0278364920987859/ASSET/9D1C8428-0D1C-417B-9448-F4DDF6250FD0/ASSETS/IMAGES/LARGE/10.1177_0278364920987859-FIG7.JPG
45. Jaiswal, A., Babu, A.R., Zadeh, M.Z., Banerjee, D., Makedon, F.: A survey on contrastive self-supervised learning. Technologies **9**, 2 (2020). https://doi.org/10.3390/TECHNOLOGIES9010002, https://www.mdpi.com/2227-7080/9/1/2/htm, https://www.mdpi.com/2227-7080/9/1/2
46. Jiang, S., Arkin, R.C.: Mixed-initiative human-robot interaction: definition, taxonomy, and survey. In: Proceedings - 2015 IEEE International Conference on Systems, Man, and Cybernetics, SMC 2015, pp. 954–961 (2016). https://doi.org/10.1109/SMC.2015.174

47. Kariyappa, S., Lécué, F., Mishra, S., Pond, C., Magazzeni, D., Veloso, M.: Progressive inference: explaining decoder-only sequence classification models using intermediate predictions (2024). https://arxiv.org/abs/2406.02625v1
48. Khoshnoodi, M., Jain, V., Gao, M., Srikanth, M., Chadha, A.: A comprehensive survey of accelerated generation techniques in large language models (2024). https://arxiv.org/abs/2405.13019v2
49. Khosla, P., et al.: Supervised contrastive learning. Adv. Neural. Inf. Process. Syst. **33**, 18661–18673 (2020)
50. Kingma, D.P., Welling, M.: An introduction to variational autoencoders. Found. Trends Mach. Learn. **12**, 307–392 (2019). https://doi.org/10.1561/2200000056
51. Krishna, S., Vuruma, R., Margetts, A., Su, J., Ahmed, F., Srivastava, B.: From cloud to edge: rethinking generative AI for low-resource design challenges (2024). https://arxiv.org/abs/2402.12702v2
52. Krishnamurthi, R., Kumar, A., Gopinathan, D., Nayyar, A., Qureshi, B.: An overview of IoT sensor data processing, fusion, and analysis techniques. Sensors **20**, 6076 (2020). https://doi.org/10.3390/S20216076
53. Lancel, K., et al.: Embrace angels: an artistic exploration of how humans and robots can embrace. In: UKAI (2025). https://nottingham-repository.worktribe.com/output/52570308. https://nottingham-repository.worktribe.com/output/52570308.abstract
54. Lancel, K., Maat, H., Brazier, F.: EEG KISS: shared multi-modal, multi brain computer interface experience, in public space. In: Nijholt, A. (ed.) Brain Art, pp. 207–228. Springer, Cham (2019). https://doi.org/10.1007/978-3-030-14323-7_7
55. Langer, M., He, Z., Rahayu, W., Xue, Y.: Distributed training of deep learning models: a taxonomic perspective. IEEE Trans. Parallel Distrib. Syst. **31**, 2802–2818 (2020). https://doi.org/10.1109/TPDS.2020.3003307
56. Lehmann, F.: Mixed-initiative interaction with computational generative systems. In: Conference on Human Factors in Computing Systems - Proceedings (2023). https://doi.org/10.1145/3544549.3577061/ASSET/73499878-D097-4382-BD19-FFEA1ECF9A4B/ASSETS/IMAGES/LARGE/CHIEA23-142-FIG1.JPG
57. Lucci, N., Lacevic, B., Zanchettin, A.M., Rocco, P.: Combining speed and separation monitoring with power and force limiting for safe collaborative robotics applications. IEEE Robot. Autom. Lett. **5**, 6121–6128 (2020). https://doi.org/10.1109/LRA.2020.3010211
58. Mathewson, K.W., Mirowski, P.: Improbotics: exploring the imitation game using machine intelligence in improvised theatre. In: Proceedings of the AAAI Conference on Artificial Intelligence and Interactive Digital Entertainment, vol. 14, pp. 59–66 (2018). https://doi.org/10.1609/AIIDE.V14I1.13030. https://ojs.aaai.org/index.php/AIIDE/article/view/13030
59. Matthews, T., et al.: Stories from survivors: privacy & security practices when coping with intimate partner abuse. In: Proceedings of the 2017 CHI Conference on Human Factors in Computing Systems, pp. 2189–2201 (2017)
60. McCormack, J., Hutchings, P., Gifford, T., Yee-King, M., Llano, M.T., D'Inverno, M.: Design considerations for real-time collaboration with creative artificial intelligence. Organised Sound **25**, 41–52 (2020). https://doi.org/10.1017/S1355771819000451
61. Mousavi, S.S., Schukat, M., Howley, E.: Deep reinforcement learning: an overview. In: Bi, Y., Kapoor, S., Bhatia, R. (eds.) IntelliSys 2016. LNNS, vol. 16, pp. 426–440. Springer, Cham (2018). https://doi.org/10.1007/978-3-319-56991-8_32

62. Nguyen, H., La, H.: Review of deep reinforcement learning for robot manipulation. In: Proceedings - 3rd IEEE International Conference on Robotic Computing, IRC 2019, pp. 590–595 (2019). https://doi.org/10.1109/IRC.2019.00120

63. Raiaan, M.A.K., et al.: A review on large language models: architectures, applications, taxonomies, open issues and challenges. IEEE Access **12**, 26839–26874 (2024). https://doi.org/10.1109/ACCESS.2024.3365742

64. Ramchurn, R., Martindale, S., Wilson, M.L., Benford, S.: From director's cut to user's cut: to watch a brain-controlled film is to edit it. In: Conference on Human Factors in Computing Systems - Proceedings (2019). https://doi.org/10.1145/3290605.3300378/SUPPL_FILE/PN4483.MP4. https://dl.acm.org/doi/10.1145/3290605.3300378

65. Ravichandar, H., Polydoros, A.S., Chernova, S., Billard, A.: Recent advances in robot learning from demonstration. Ann. Rev. Control Robot. Auton. Syst. **3**, 297–330 (2020). https://doi.org/10.1146/ANNUREV-CONTROL-100819-063206/CITE/REFWORKS

66. Redifer, J.L., Bae, C.L., Zhao, Q.: Self-efficacy and performance feedback: impacts on cognitive load during creative thinking. Learn. Instr. **71**, 101395 (2021). https://doi.org/10.1016/J.LEARNINSTRUC.2020.101395

67. Rincon, R.A.D.: Generating music and generative art from brain activity (2021). https://arxiv.org/abs/2108.04316v2

68. Salwa, H., Burhan, N., Rahel, E.: Continual learning: overcoming catastrophic forgetting for adaptive ai systems. Authorea Preprints (2025). https://doi.org/10.36227/techrxiv.173886426.63028528/v1

69. Saunders, R., Gemeinboeck, P.: Creative AI, embodiment, and performance. Springer Series on Cultural Computing, pp. 191–206 (2022). https://doi.org/10.1007/978-3-031-10960-7_11

70. Sengar, S.S., Hasan, A.B., Kumar, S., Carroll, F.: Generative artificial intelligence: a systematic review and applications. Multimedia Tools Appl. **84**, 23661–23700 (2025). https://doi.org/10.1007/S11042-024-20016-1/TABLES/9

71. Sexton, T.: Musenet. Music Ref. Serv. Q. **26**, 151–153 (2023). https://doi.org/10.1080/10588167.2023.2247289

72. Shiri, F.M., Perumal, T., Mustapha, N., Mohamed, R.: A comprehensive overview and comparative analysis on deep learning models: CNN, RNN, LSTM, GRU. J. Artif. Intell. **6**, 301–360 (2025). https://doi.org/10.32604/jai.2024.054314

73. Sun, W., et al.: Speed always wins: a survey on efficient architectures for large language models (2025). https://arxiv.org/abs/2508.09834v1

74. Suresh, R., Tomar, V.: Self-supervised learning in generative AI: a game changer for creativity. Int. J. Comput. Technol. Electron. Commun. **2**, 1206–1211 (2019). https://doi.org/10.15680/IJCTECE.2019.0203002

75. Svarny, P., Tesar, M., Behrens, J.K., Hoffmann, M.: Safe physical HRI: toward a unified treatment of speed and separation monitoring together with power and force limiting. In: IEEE International Conference on Intelligent Robots and Systems, pp. 7580–7587 (2019). https://doi.org/10.1109/IROS40897.2019.8968463

76. Tang, Q., Liang, J., Zhu, F.: A comparative review on multi-modal sensors fusion based on deep learning. Signal Process. **213**, 109165 (2023). https://doi.org/10.1016/J.SIGPRO.2023.109165

77. Tang, Z., Wang, X., Wu, J., Ping, Y., Guo, X., Cui, Z.: A BCI painting system using a hybrid control approach based on ssvep and p300. Comput. Biol. Med. **150**, 106118 (2022). https://doi.org/10.1016/J.COMPBIOMED.2022.106118

78. Thorn, O., Knudsen, P., Saffiotti, A.: Human-robot artistic co-creation: a study in improvised robot dance. In: 29th IEEE International Conference on Robot and Human Interactive Communication, RO-MAN 2020, pp. 845–850 (2020). https://doi.org/10.1109/RO-MAN47096.2020.9223446
79. Tian, Y., et al.: What makes for good views for contrastive learning? Adv. Neural. Inf. Process. Syst. **33**, 6827–6839 (2020)
80. Vaswani, A., et al.: Attention is all you need. Adv. Neural Inf. Process. Syst. **30** (2017)
81. Wadeson, A., Nijholt, A., Nam, C.S.: Artistic brain-computer interfaces: state-of-the-art control mechanisms. Brain-Comput. Interfaces **2**, 70–75 (2015). https://doi.org/10.1080/2326263X.2015.1103155
82. Wang, Y., Yao, Q., Kwok, J.T., Ni, L.M.: Generalizing from a few examples. ACM Comput. Surv. (CSUR) **53** (2020). https://doi.org/10.1145/3386252
83. Wang, Y., Blei, D.M., Cunningham, J.P.: Posterior collapse and latent variable non-identifiability. Adv. Neural Inf. Process. Syst. **7**, 5443–5455 (2023). https://arxiv.org/abs/2301.00537v1
84. Wickramasinghe, B., Saha, G., Roy, K.: Continual learning: a review of techniques, challenges, and future directions. IEEE Trans. Artif. Intell. **5**, 2526–2546 (2024). https://doi.org/10.1109/TAI.2023.3339091
85. Winston, L., Magerko, B.: Turn-taking with improvisational co-creative agents. In: Proceedings of the AAAI Conference on Artificial Intelligence and Interactive Digital Entertainment, vol. 13, pp. 129–135 (2017). https://doi.org/10.1609/AIIDE.V13I1.12931
86. Woodward, K., Kanjo, E.: ifidgetcube: tangible fidgeting interfaces (tfis) to monitor and improve mental wellbeing. IEEE Sensors J. (2020). https://doi.org/10.1109/JSEN.2020.3031163. https://ieeexplore.ieee.org/document/9223707/
87. Woodward, K., Kanjo, E.: Parallel feature fusion for multimodal scene recognition on dual-core MCUs. IEEE Pervasive Comput. (2025). https://doi.org/10.1109/MPRV.2025.3555334
88. Woodward, K., et al.: Beyond mobile apps: a survey of technologies for mental well-being. IEEE Trans. Affect. Comput. (2020)
89. Woodward, K., Kanjo, E., Brown, D.J., McGinnity, T.: Towards personalised mental wellbeing recognition on-device using transfer learning "in the wild". In: IEEE International Smart Cities Conference 2021 (2021)
90. Woodward, K., Kanjo, E., Tsanas, A.: Combining deep transfer learning and signal-image encoding for multi-modal mental wellbeing classification. Submitted to Information Fusion (2021)
91. Wu, Z., Pan, S., Chen, F., Long, G., Zhang, C., Yu, P.S.: A comprehensive survey on graph neural networks. IEEE Trans. Neural Netw. Learn. Syst. **32**, 4–24 (2021). https://doi.org/10.1109/TNNLS.2020.2978386
92. Yin, W., Yin, H., Baraka, K., Kragic, D., Björkman, M.: Dance style transfer with cross-modal transformer. In: Proceedings of the IEEE/CVF Winter Conference on Applications of Computer Vision (WACV), 2023, pp. 5058–5067 (2023)
93. Yin, W., Yin, H., Kragic, D., Bjorkman, M.: Graph-based normalizing flow for human motion generation and reconstruction. In: 2021 30th IEEE International Conference on Robot and Human Interactive Communication, RO-MAN 2021, pp. 641–648 (2021). https://doi.org/10.1109/RO-MAN50785.2021.9515316
94. Zander, T.O., Kothe, C.: Towards passive brain–computer interfaces: applying brain–computer interface technology to human–machine systems in general. J. Neural Eng. **8**, 025005 (2011). https://doi.org/10.1088/1741-2560/8/2/025005

95. Zhang, C., Xie, Y., Bai, H., Yu, B., Li, W., Gao, Y.: A survey on federated learning. Knowl.-Based Syst. **216**, 106775 (2021). https://doi.org/10.1016/J.KNOSYS.2021.106775

96. Zhao, W., Gangaraju, K., Yuan, F.: Multimodal perception-driven decision-making for human-robot interaction: a survey. Front. Robot. AI **12**, 1604472 (2025). https://doi.org/10.3389/FROBT.2025.1604472/BIBTEX

97. Zhao, Y., Yang, R., Chevalier, G., Xu, X., Zhang, Z.: Deep residual Bidir-LSTM for human activity recognition using wearable sensors. Math. Probl. Eng. **2018** (2018). https://doi.org/10.1155/2018/7316954

98. Zhou, Z., et al.: A survey on efficient inference for large language models (2024). https://arxiv.org/abs/2404.14294v3

99. Zhuang, F., et al.: A comprehensive survey on transfer learning. Proc. IEEE **109**, 43–76 (2021). https://doi.org/10.1109/JPROC.2020.3004555

100. Ziv, A., et al.: Masked audio generation using a single non-autoregressive transformer. In: 12th International Conference on Learning Representations, ICLR 2024 (2024). https://arxiv.org/abs/2401.04577v2

Creative AI for Live Performance

An Artistic BCI–GenAI System Enabling Real-Time Co-creation in Balinese Performance

Aime J. Aguilar-Herrera[1(✉)] [iD], Carlos O. Hernández-Aguado[1,2] [iD],
Joel A. Monarres-Sokolovskaya[1,2] [iD], Maxine Annel Pacheco-Ramírez[1] [iD],
Badie Khaleghian[3,6] [iD], Elena Grassi[1] [iD], Made Ayu Desiari[4] [iD],
I Gde Made Indra Sadguna[4] [iD], Cokorda Bagus Jaya Lesmana[5] [iD],
Anthony Brandt[6] [iD], and Jose L. Contreras Vidal[1(✉)] [iD]

[1] IUCRC BRAIN, Cullen College of Engineering, University of Houston, Houston,
USA
ajaguil3@CougarNet.UH.EDU, mpachec4@cougarnet.uh.edu,
{egrassi3,jlcontreras-vidal}@uh.edu
[2] Science and Engineering School, Tecnológico de Monterrey, Monterrey, Mexico
[3] Now at Bowdoin College, Brunswick, USA
b.khaleghian@bowdoin.edu
[4] Indonesian Institute of the Arts Denpasar, Denpasar, Indonesia
indra_sadguna@yahoo.com
[5] Faculty of Medicine, Udayana University, Denpasar, Indonesia
cokordabagus@unud.ac.id
[6] Shepherd School of Music, Rice University, Houston, USA
abrandt@rice.edu

Abstract. This study presents a cross-cultural implementation of an artistic Brain–Computer Interface (BCI) and generative artificial intelligence (GenAI) system designed for live performance within the Balinese gamelan tradition. The BCI-GenAI system enables real-time translation of neural synchrony between dyads of performers (musician-musician, dancer-dancer, musician-dancer) into the control of culturally-relevant generative visual projections that interact with performers and audience alike. Nine Balinese artists (six musicians and three dancers) participated in a two-part performance *Janaki Dewi: Sita's Reverie* and *Wiwada Manik: Tales of the Brothers*. Dyads of artists wore Mobile Brain-Body Imaging (MoBI) technology to capture in real time their brain (electroencephalography, EEG) and ocular (electrooculography, EOG) activities, head motion, and video during rehearsals and a public performance over a period of 3 weeks. All signals were synchronized by hardware. A Brain-Computer Interface (BCI) preprocessed the MoBI Signals and computed the inter-brain synchrony between dyads. Synchrony indices derived from EEG bispectra modulated diffusion parameters in a StreamDiffusion-based GenAI, whereas text prompts consisting of culturally-relevant narrative and emotional descriptors reflected the story's mythological and affective dimensions. Thus, the BCI-GenAI system linked the real-time inter-brain synchronization to dynamic imagery projected live on stage.

© The Author(s), under exclusive license to Springer Nature Switzerland AG 2026

K. Woodward et al. (Eds.): CLIP 2026, CCIS 2865, pp. 25–41, 2026.
https://doi.org/10.1007/978-3-032-16893-1_2

The system thus functioned as a creative partner in-the-loop, responsive to both the emotional and rhythmic structure of performance. The multi-institutional, cross-cultural project contributes a methodological framework for BCI-GenAI in artistic settings, emphasizing cross-cultural collaboration, the symbiosis between cultural traditions and emergent technologies, and ethical data governance. It advances a model of responsible human–AI co-creation, where technology supports rather than displaces tradition thereby preserving the continuity of cultural identity through innovation, team science and transdisciplinarity.

Keywords: Brain–Computer Interface (BCI) · Mobile Brain–Body Imaging (MoBI) · Generative Artificial Intelligence (GenAI) · Real-Time Signal Processing · Human–AI Co-Creation · Neuroaesthetics · Human–Centered AI · AI for Culture and Heritage

1   Introduction

In recent years, artificial intelligence has progressed from being a static tool of creative production to a dynamic collaborator capable of shaping, interpreting, and co-creating in real time. Whereas early applications of AI in art often treated the machine as a one-way executor of human ideas, the next frontier lies in interactive intelligence: systems that do not merely execute instructions but engage in the improvisational flow of human expression. Such systems must learn to "listen" to respond dynamically to human input, adapt to changing social and environmental contexts, and therefore facilitate ongoing human–AI collaboration during performance [7].

This shift from automation to interaction marks a fundamental rethinking of creativity as a two-way system rather than a linear pipeline. In live performance contexts, the creative act is inherently reciprocal: a dancer adjusts to the rhythm of a drum; a musician interprets audience energy; an ensemble synchronizes through gaze, breath, and anticipation [1]. For an AI system to participate meaningfully, it must move beyond pattern recognition toward embodied awareness, interpreting the fluid, often ambiguous cues that underpin artistic communication [10].

1.1   The Balinese Gamelan

Balinese gamelan music provides a compelling ethnomusicological framework for examining collective intelligence and emergent synchrony in ensemble performance. Its interlocking rhythmic structures (*kotekan*), cyclical temporal organization, and fluid ensemble coordination embody the Balinese philosophical triad of Tri Hita Karana—harmony among the divine (*parahyangan*), humanity (*pawongan*), and nature (palemahan) [15]. In contrast to most Western orchestral traditions, each gamelan ensemble is uniquely tuned and transmitted through oral pedagogy rather than written notation; musicians acquire proficiency through processes of memory, imitation, and communal rehearsal [9, 14].

Performance, therefore, becomes a social act of embodied cognition, in which individual agency is subsumed within a shared sensorimotor framework. The resulting musical expression exemplifies an art form where technical virtuosity and intersubjective synchrony are inseparable. The interdependent texture of gamelan's rhythmic stratification necessitates constant cooperation, adaptation, and mutual entrainment among participants [17], positioning gamelan as an ideal empirical paradigm for investigating real-time mutual adaptation and distributed creativity in complex cultural systems.

1.2   Interactive Performance and the BCI-GenAI Paradigm

Recent advances in Brain–Computer Interface (BCI) technology enable such real-time monitoring of a user's cognitive and emotional states, allowing interactive systems to dynamically adapt to the person's internal state [16]. In this study, we developed an artistic BCI-GenAI environment integrated into a live Balinese performance. Neural signals from the performing dyads were captured and analyzed in real time, providing the AI system with continuous information about the level of brain synchronization. The AI transformed these inputs into dynamic visual outputs, grounded in the Balinese cultural traditions, to support the performance.

Related work integrating hyperscanning and real-time BCI in artistic or performance contexts is still limited but provides important precedents for our approach. Prior MoBI and hyperscanning studies have examined inter-brain coupling during dance [18], theatrical acting [5], and collaborative movement and music improvisation [12]. However, these studies primarily focus on Western artistic frameworks—classical chamber music, jazz improvisation, and contemporary concert dance—reflecting a broader tendency in the neuroscience of music to overlook non-Western traditions. Recent reviews of musical hyperscanning consistently exclude traditional or Indigenous music cultures, revealing a geographic and cultural imbalance in the field [2]. Our work addresses this gap by embedding real-time BCI within a culturally grounded Balinese gamelan context, extending neural performance research into a ritual and aesthetic system largely absent from existing studies. This approach not only contributes to the diversification of hyperscanning-based research but also invites broader reflection on how co-performance and neural synchrony manifest in diverse musical ontologies.

Three themes guided the design and interpretation of this environment: first, how an AI might respond to the internal states of highly skilled collaborative gamelan artists; second, how such responsiveness could foster genuine collaboration integrating cultural traditions and emergent technologies to advance understanding of the creative and social brains in action; and third, how we might evaluate creativity in systems where success depends not on precision but on resonance—where the measure of intelligence is the ability to promote understanding.

1.3 Cultural and Ethical Dimensions of Co-creation

The inclusion of neural data and AI-generated media in cultural performance raises questions that are as ethical as they are technical. Neural data are deeply personal and artistic traditions are socially situated; when technology enters these domains, the issues of consent, ownership, and reciprocity must be reconsidered [19]. Who owns a creative output co-generated by human physiology and algorithmic inference? How can we safeguard the dignity of communities whose cultural heritage becomes data? [3, 11].

In the Balinese context, where art functions as a form of devotion and social cohesion, such questions are inseparable from cultural ethics. We argue that co-creative AI systems must be designed with principles of cultural stewardship—ensuring that they amplify, rather than appropriate, local traditions.

This study contributes to the understanding of human–AI co-creation through an integrated, cross-cultural experiment in the performing arts. It presents an artistic BCI–GenAI framework deployed within a Balinese gamelan setting, demonstrating how traditional ensemble structures can inform the design and deployment of adaptive algorithms. It also proposes a framework for evaluating creative interaction that balances quantitative measures of synchrony with qualitative assessments of aesthetic and cultural resonance.

2 Methods

The study was conducted in collaboration with faculty and students from the Institut Seni Indonesia (ISI) Denpasar and researchers from the University of Houston, Rice University, and Udayana University. Nine Balinese performers (six musicians and three dancers) all students of ISI Denpasar participated in the recordings. All participants provided informed consent and signed media release forms prior to data collection under the approved institutional protocol Your Brain on Dance approved by the Institutional Review Boards at the University of Houston, Rice University and Udayana University.

The performance took place in the Udayana University Faculty of Medicine Auditorium after a sequence of thirteen rehearsals held at ISI Denpasar. The performance was open to faculty and local community members, serving as both a research experiment and a live cultural event.

The artistic program drew from two Balinese narrative works: *Janaki Dewi: Sita's Reverie* and *Wiwada Manik: Tales of the Brothers*, composed by I Gde Made Indra Sadguna and choreographed by Made Ayu Desiari. The first depicts Sita's emotional and spiritual longing for reunion with her husband, while the second portrays two brothers transformed into monkeys after discovering a magical stone. Together, these stories symbolically explore the feminine and masculine, the emotional and physical, and the earthly and spiritual—paralleling the system's dual exploration of human and artificial creativity (Fig. 1).

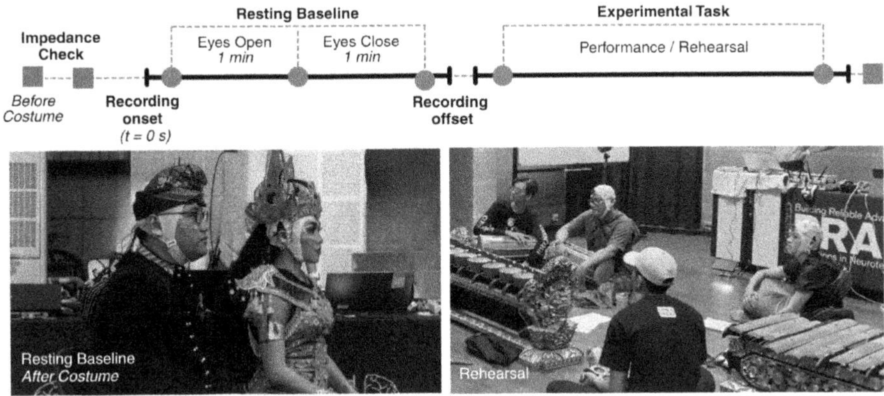

Fig. 1. Experimental protocol and setup. Top: Timeline of the experimental procedure, including impedance checks, resting-state baselines (eyes open and closed, 1 min each), and the performance/rehearsal task. Bottom left: Resting baseline acquisition after performers donned traditional costumes. Bottom right: Rehearsal with active EEG acquisition and synchronized recording of musicians and dancers prior to the live performance.

2.1   Mobile Brain-Body Imaging Set Up

Neural and motion data were recorded using a 28-channel actiCAP EEG system (Brain Products GmbH, Germany) following the international 10–20 system, supplemented by 4 electrooculography (EOG) channels and a 9-axis IMU integrated into the head module. Impedances were maintained below 50 kΩ, and in most cases below 25 kΩ (Figs. 2 and 3).

For the female lead dancer, electrode configuration was modified due to the traditional gelungan (headdress), which exerted variable pressure on frontal and temporal electrodes during movement. To reduce noise and ensure comfort while maintaining anatomical validity, the F7/F8 electrodes were repositioned to correspond approximately with T7/T8, while CP5/CP6 and PO7/PO8 were adjusted for improved temporal and occipital coverage. This configuration preserved symmetry and compliance with 10–20 spatial conventions while mitigating impedance variability caused by motion and headgear. EEG and EOG were sampled at 1 kHz, IMU data at 128 Hz, and synchronized audiovisual recordings at 30 frames per second, aligned via hardware triggers from the laboratory's custom SyncBox.

2.2   BCI GenAI Framework

In the first segment of the public performance, *Janaki Dewi: Sita's Reverie*, the female lead dancer and the principal drummer formed the BCI pair. In the second segment, *Wiwada Manik: Tales of the Brothers*, the principal drummer and the secondary drummer became the active pair. The real-time visualization

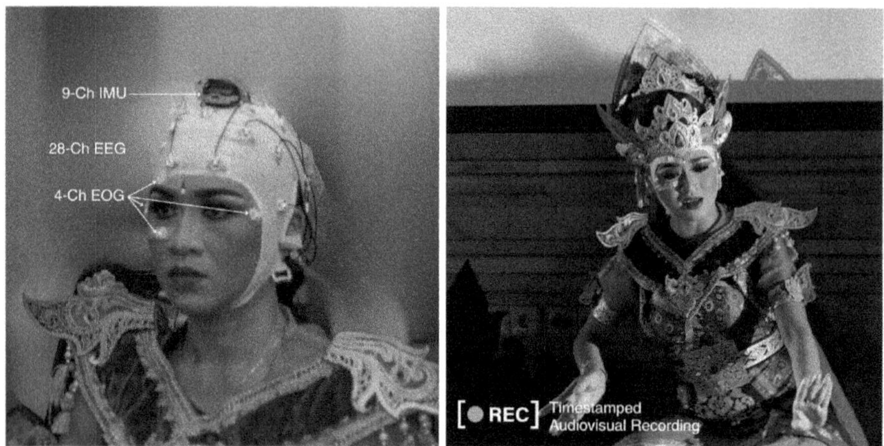

Fig. 2. EEG configuration and synchronized audiovisual recording. MoBI set up integrated 28 EEG channels, 4 EOG channels, and a 9-axis IMU mounted atop the head module for motion tracking before the performance. The right panel shows the live Sita's Reverie performance recorded with timestamped audiovisual feeds synchronized via hardware triggers. The EEG system was discreetly embedded within the dancer's costume, preserving cultural authenticity and visual harmony while enabling unobtrusive, high-fidelity neural data collection during live performance.

system was implemented as an adaptive, closed-loop architecture linking neural synchrony, movement, and generative visual output. Two performer dyads served as the primary neural sources for the system, corresponding to the narrative structure of the performance.

Figure 4 illustrates the real-time processing pipeline. EEG signals were first denoised using H-infinity filtering to suppress ocular and movement artifacts [8], followed by band-pass filtering (1–49 Hz), Laplacian spatial filtering, and computation of a synchrony index based on bispectral analysis [13]. Inter-brain synchrony between dyads of performers was estimated across eight homologous channels (Fp1, Fp2, C3, C4, P3, P4, O1, O2) in the gamma band, using the bispectrum defined as:

$$B(f_1, f_2) = E[X(f_1) \cdot X(f_2) \cdot X^*(f_1 + f_2)],$$

where $X(f)$ is the Fourier transform of the EEG signal and X^* its complex conjugate. This nonlinear spectral approach captures quadratic phase coupling and was selected for its robustness in dynamic, real-world performance settings.

The real-time projection system was implemented in TouchDesigner 2023 [6] using an NVIDIA RTX 4090 GPU. Brain synchrony indices were transmitted to the visualization engine via a TCP connection over a wired Ethernet network at a rate of 2 Hz, smoothed over a 250 ms window to minimize abrupt transitions. The system continuously monitored the synchrony range over 25 s intervals, dynam-

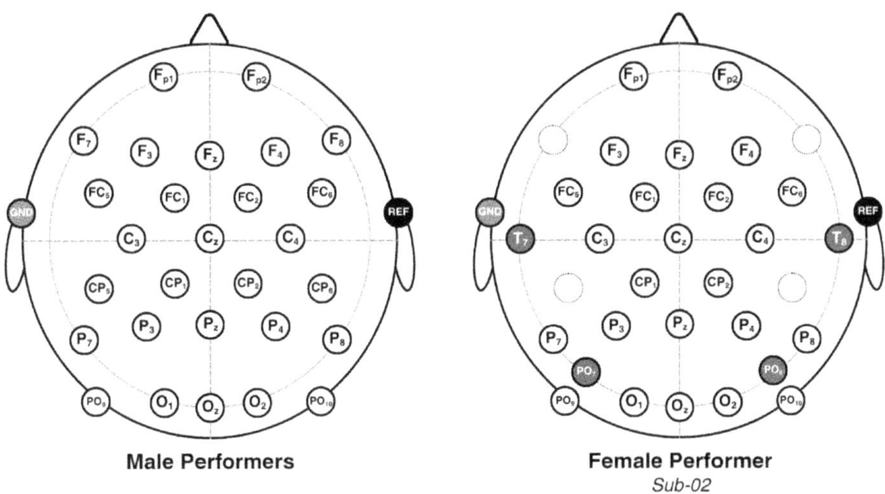

Fig. 3. The 28-channel EEG layout followed the international 10–20 system. Left: Standard configuration. Right: Modified configuration for the female dancer, in which the F7/F8 electrodes were repositioned to T7/T8, and CP5/CP6 and PO7/PO8 were shifted to reduce impedance variability caused by the gelungan (headdress) while maintaining spatial symmetry.

ically adjusting scaling to accommodate changes in signal amplitude across the performance.

A 3D sphere generated with TouchDesigner's Sphere SOP and Noise SOP operators served as the base visual element. Rotation velocity, color intensity, and surface deformation were parameterized by synchrony level. High synchrony produced increased rotational speed and high-frequency surface noise, resulting in a more complex texture, whereas low synchrony reduced rotation and smoothed the surface topology.

During *Janaki Dewi: Sita's Reverie*, the sphere employed a uniform material whose hue shifted continuously with synchrony values. In *Wiwada Manik: Tales of the Brothers*, the sphere was divided into red and blue hemispheres representing the two principal characters.

The animated sphere frames were used as input to a StreamDiffusion img2img pipeline operating at 512×512 px resolution with a transformation strength of approximately 0.5, preserving the spatial structure while introducing stylistic augmentation from text-based prompts. Prompts were updated manually at key choreographic and musical transitions, defined in collaboration with the composer and choreographer to align visual output with narrative and emotional structure.

Following generation, StreamDiffusion outputs underwent additional 2D post-processing with fluid-based visual effects before being upscaled to 4K resolution for projection. The total system latency (from data acquisition to rendered

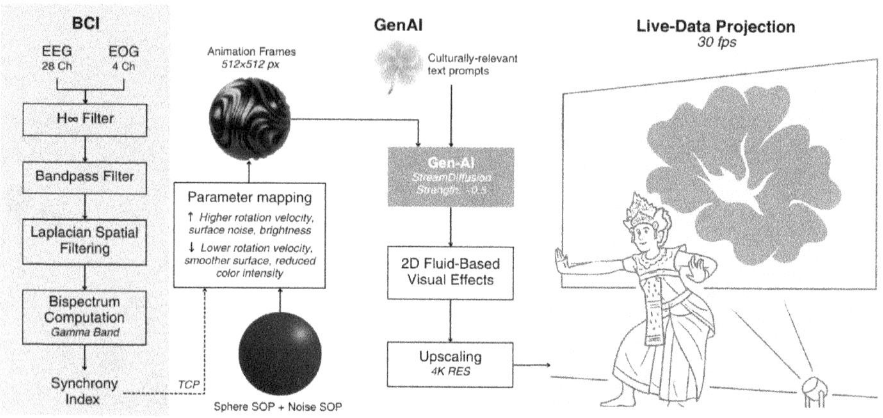

Fig. 4. EEG from performer dyads were processed in real time to compute synchrony indices that modulated parameters of a StreamDiffusion generative model, which was setup using culturally-relevant text prompts. The AI output, composited in TouchDesigner, was projected live, completing the feedback loop between performer state and visual expression.

projection) averaged 160 ms at 30 fps, providing a perceptually continuous and temporally coherent response to real-time performer states.

In the first piece, *Janaki Dewi: Sita's Reverie*, the visual projection opens on a solitary gong resonating in an empty room. This image evokes the moment of Sita's capture and imprisonment—an act of separation and confinement, setting the emotional stage for her memory of reunion. At the moment when the singing transforms into remembrance and longing for reunion, the projection shifts to a vibrant bloom of the Balinese "mekar kembang" flower (specifically the kembang jepun), symbolising her inner liberation and the blooming of joy as she recalls the promise of return.

In the second piece, *Wiwada Manik: Tales of the Brothers*, the visual projection begins with a set of stylised Balinese stone-sculpture forms presented during the moment when the two brothers discover the stone and the conflict emerges. At this stage, the generative outputs incorporate red and blue tonal regions, corresponding to the identities of the two brothers and visually maintaining their distinction prior to transformation. When the performers execute the costume change (from human attire into monkey-costumes) the projection transitions into imagery depicting monkey-like figures. These figures are rendered as paired forms that preserve the brothers' red–blue identity contrast while representing their transformation into monkey-beings consistent with the narrative arc.

3   Interaction Paradigms and Collaboration Models

This project was grounded in a team science framework, bringing together collaborators from neuroscience, AI, neurology, ethnomusicology, dance, and digital arts. The interdisciplinary team included students and researchers from

Indonesia, and the United States, co-creating each stage of the process from ideation to implementation. Such an approach emphasized reciprocity and mutual respect, ensuring the project was not merely extracting data from a cultural tradition, but contributing to it.

Rather than treating AI as a tool for automation, the system was designed as a co-adaptive partner in the creative process. The GenAI system responded to the neuro-physiological signals of the performers, while the artists, who were seated in front of the visual GenAI projections in the final performance, likely adapted in real-time to visual output generated by the AI. In this regard, the BCI-GenAI system functioned as a user-in-the-loop co-creative system.

4   Results

Neural synchrony between performer pairs revealed distinct temporal patterns corresponding to narrative and interaction type. During *Janaki Dewi: Sita's Reverie* (Sub-01 & Sub-02), high inter-brain synchrony emerged during emotionally resonant, slow-tempo passages when the dancer and principal drummer engaged in gaze exchange and mirrored breathing rhythms. In contrast, *Wiwada Manik: Tales of the Brothers* (Sub-01 & Sub-03) exhibited peaks of synchrony during high-energy percussive coordination, particularly in moments of call-and-response drumming.

The real-time generative system responded dynamically to these fluctuations (Fig. 5). Under low synchrony conditions, visuals displayed, small ratio, smooth unified diffusion patterns, characterized by coherent color blending and slower spatial evolution. In contrast, high synchrony intervals produced high entropy and rapid color transitions. These transitions occurred continuously throughout the live performance, aligning with both narrative tension and ensemble dynamics.

Preliminary observations were derived from real-time signal processing, while offline analyses are currently being conducted to confirm the temporal correspondence between synchrony fluctuations and visual transitions, as well as to quantify phase-locking and cross-spectral coupling across dyads.

5   Discussion

5.1   Evaluation of Co-creative Performance Systems

Evaluating interactive AI systems within live cultural performance requires frameworks that extend beyond conventional technical metrics. In this study, performance success was defined not by algorithmic precision but by aesthetic coherence, emotional resonance, and cultural authenticity. The coupling between inter-brain synchrony and generative visuals demonstrated that neural coordination can serve as a meaningful input for co-creative systems, allowing artistic expression to emerge through shared physiological states.

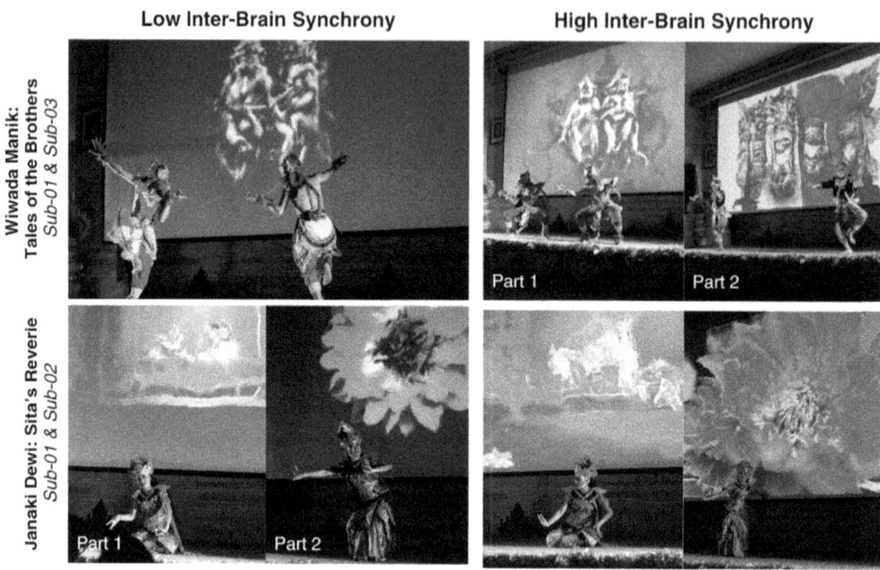

Fig. 5. Inter-brain synchrony and adaptive generative visualization across performance segments. Representative frames from Janaki Dewi: Sita's Reverie (bottom) and Wiwada Manik: Tales of the Brothers (top) illustrate low (left) and high (right) interbrain synchrony states between performer dyads. Brain synchrony dynamically modulated the StreamDiffusion-based generative visuals: high synchrony yielded smooth, luminous imagery; low synchrony produced fragmented, high-contrast textures.

Post-performance reflections supported this finding: both dancers and musicians reported that the visual projections "moved with their rhythm," while audience members perceived the imagery as "breathing with the music." These experiences suggest that measurable synchrony may align with subjective states of artistic flow, providing a bridge between physiological coordination and aesthetic perception.

Future evaluations will integrate quantitative synchrony metrics with qualitative ethnographic analysis—including performer interviews and audience feedback—to create a multidimensional framework for assessing human–AI co-creation.

A potential extension of this system involves enabling the GenAI to autonomously recognize and adapt to narrative shifts. While the current framework uses intentional prompt updates aligned with choreographic structure, future work may explore models that learn the temporal, emotional, and dramaturgical signatures of Balinese performance, allowing the AI to adjust its generative style without manual intervention. Such narrative-aware adaptation would further enhance the system's creative agency and responsiveness.

5.2   The Artistic Co-creation System as Distributed Intelligence

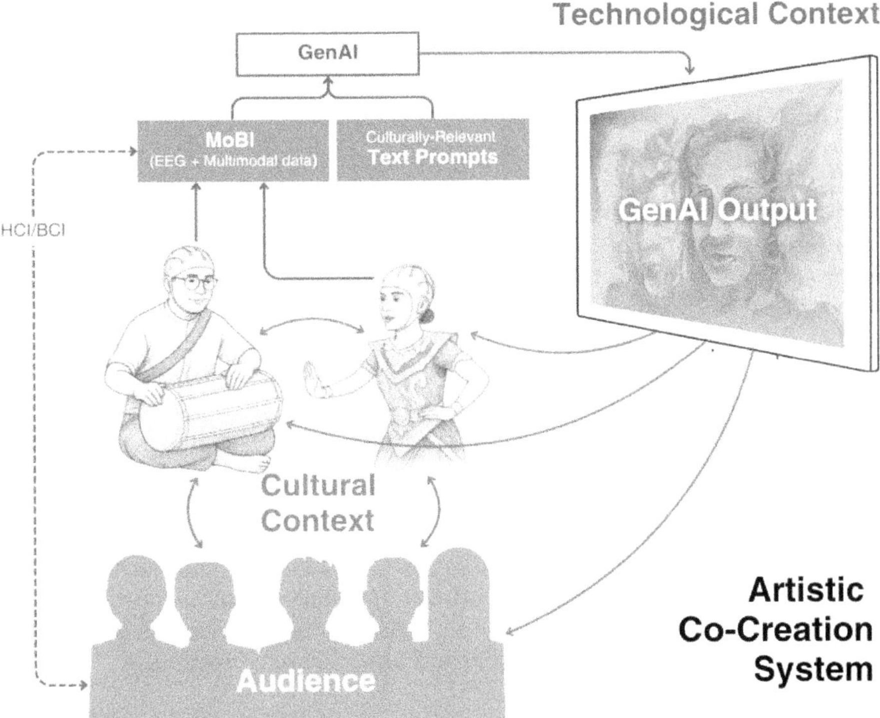

Fig. 6. Diagram of the Artistic Co-Creation System integrating technological (blue) and cultural (orange) contexts. The technological context includes the Mobile Brain-Body Imaging (MoBI) system, which records EEG and multimodal data from performers, and the Generative AI (GenAI) model, which receives both neural signals and culturally relevant text prompts to generate dynamic visual outputs. The cultural context encompasses the performers, audience, and narrative elements that shape and interpret the co-creative process. The orange arrows represent the flow of cultural meaning and perceptual feedback—auditory and visual perception of the GenAI output—while the dotted blue line indicates a potential extension of human–computer/brain–computer interfaces (HCI/BCI) to audiences, enabling participatory and collective engagement in real time. (Color figure online)

The Artistic Co-Creation System (Fig. 6) situates performance within a broader network of human, computational, and cultural interactions. In this framework, artists—the dancer and drummers—contribute real-time brain and motion data via BCIs, capturing physiological and cognitive traces of expression. Simultaneously, the audience becomes an active participant through Human–Computer Interfaces (HCI) such as affective sensing, gaze tracking, or interactive projection mapping. These human inputs collectively inform the generative AI, which translates them into evolving audiovisual responses.

The resulting feedback loops connect the performers' neural and bodily states, the AI's adaptive outputs, and the audience's perceptual engagement, all within a shared cultural context that governs meaning and interpretation. This distributed model re-frames creativity as a collective cognitive process, emerging from dynamic exchanges among biological, artificial, and social agents. Rather than viewing AI as a tool of automation, this system positions it as a participant in cultural cognition—a responsive collaborator that interprets, adapts, and co-evolves with its human counterparts.

During the post-performance Q&A session, several audience members emphasized that the system did more than translate neural activity into visuals—it contributed to a sense of cultural revitalization. They described the experience as "bringing the old and the new together," noting that the integration of AI made ancestral narratives feel newly accessible to younger audiences. Rather than perceiving the technology as disruptive, viewers expressed that it extended the cultural reach of Balinese performance, offering a contemporary layer that complemented rather than displaced the traditional choreography and music. These reflections suggest that co-creative neuro-AI systems may serve as vehicles for cultural continuity, enabling traditional forms to resonate with emerging generations.

The event sparked interdisciplinary curiosity among artists, students, and faculty, leading to follow-up discussions about potential applications of this framework in ethnomusicology, digital arts, psychology, and education. These reactions highlight the project's role not only as a technological demonstration but as a catalyst for cultural dialogue and new research directions.

5.3   Technical and Methodological Challenges

Implementing MoBI and AI visualization in a live, ritualized performance introduced several technical and logistical challenges. The combination of dense EEG recording, continuous movement, heat, and traditional attire required meticulous system calibration and real-time artifact management. Wearability, comfort, and visual discretion were essential to maintain both artistic integrity and data quality. Custom adhesives and low-profile wiring were engineered to integrate seamlessly into the dancer's costume, demonstrating how cultural and aesthetic constraints can directly inspire technological innovation.

A particular consideration involved the placement of EOG electrodes within the dancer's makeup design, which was a fundamental element of the performance's visual identity. To preserve the integrity of the makeup while ensuring high-quality recordings, stickers were first applied around the eye area to define electrode placement. The interior of each sticker was then carefully cleaned with cotton swabs, makeup remover, and alcohol before the electrodes were affixed. Although this procedure deviated from conventional laboratory preparation, it provided stable impedance and reliable signal quality without compromising the dancer's appearance or comfort.

These adaptive techniques illustrate the importance of context-specific engineering when conducting MoBI in real-world artistic environments, where scientific rigor must coexist with the expressive and cultural demands of performance.

5.4 Data Annotation, Standardization, and Reuse

Despite significant advances, no standardized framework currently exists for labeling or structuring event data in MoBI or BCI research. Human-centered datasets that employ comprehensive Hierarchical Event Descriptor (HED) annotations are rare, limiting interoperability and cross-study comparison. The present dataset contributes to this growing effort by adopting BIDS-compatible structure and HED-based labeling for events such as musical transitions, movement cues, and generative AI triggers.

However, broader adoption requires community-level coordination and long-term infrastructure investment. Open repositories must also accommodate audio-visual and creative content, which often falls under copyright or cultural protection. These materials are indispensable for contextual interpretation but present legal and ethical challenges in open science frameworks. Developing repositories that balance data accessibility with cultural and intellectual property rights will be essential for the sustainable growth of artistic neuroscience.

Our forthcoming open dataset will include synchronized EEG, EOG, IMU, audio, and annotated video segments aligned with the narrative structure of both performances. Metadata will follow BIDS and HED conventions to support interoperability across cultural and artistic neuroscience domains. Additionally, we are preparing narrative-aligned prompt lists and generative AI configuration files to enable future researchers to replicate or extend the co-creative pipeline.

5.5 Ethical, Legal, and Cultural Considerations

As AI and neurotechnology enter artistic and public domains, they confront unresolved ethical and legal complexities. Performers—often public figures or cultural bearers—possess privacy, authorship, and publicity rights that extend beyond standard research subjects. In this project, ethical compliance was ensured through transparent consent, anonymization of physiological data, and co-authorship with the Institut Seni Indonesia (ISI) Denpasar collaborators.

Cultural sensitivity was embedded from the outset: a choreographer provided narrative and symbolic input that guided the AI's visual generation process, ensuring the projections remained faithful to the storylines of Sita's Reverie and Wiwada Manik. This participatory model prevented algorithmic misrepresentation and emphasized reciprocity and respect. The resulting integration of AI into a traditional art form preserved cultural meaning while demonstrating that technology can reinforce rather than disrupt heritage when designed collaboratively. Nonetheless, broader institutional frameworks must evolve to safeguard artistic identity, authorship, and community data ownership as such interdisciplinary projects proliferate.

In alignment with emerging frameworks for ethical data governance, this project also acknowledges the work of the IEEE P2895 Standard Taxonomy for Responsible Use and Privacy of Human-Generated Data [4], which defines a taxonomy for the transparent description of data rights, permitted and restricted uses, exceptions, duration, and jurisdiction of processing. Such international efforts provide a foundation for responsibly managing human and cultural data in interdisciplinary, creative AI research.

5.6 Sustainability and Infrastructural Challenges

MoBI-based artistic research remains constrained by the short-term nature of academic funding. Equipment maintenance, technical expertise, and interdisciplinary training demand sustained investment rarely supported by current grant models. Building open-source, reusable pipelines and datasets is a step toward democratization, but long-term success requires institutional structures that value the cultural as well as scientific impact of this work.

Cross-institutional collaboration between universities, art academies, and cultural organizations could provide the foundation for shared infrastructure and distributed knowledge networks, ensuring that both hardware and cultural expertise remain accessible for future research.

5.7 Toward Responsible AI for Cultural Continuity

The integration of AI and neurotechnology into traditional practices offers a path not only toward innovation but toward cultural preservation through transformation. When technological systems are co-designed with local artists and grounded in cultural frameworks, they help sustain collective identity and ensure continuity across generations.

The Balinese case study demonstrates that respectful implementation of creative AI can extend the life of tradition by embedding it in new forms of expression, rather than extracting or replacing it. Ultimately, this work advocates for a paradigm of responsible co-creation, where AI is evaluated not only by technical performance but by its capacity to foster empathy, inclusivity, and cultural vitality.

6 Conclusion

Future research will expand upon the present framework by deepening the integration between neural, behavioral, and affective data within multimodal creative systems. Ongoing work includes offline analysis of inter-brain synchrony, cross-frequency coupling, and motion alignment to validate real-time findings and refine models of co-adaptive creativity. Efforts are also underway to develop open-access pipelines for cultural MoBI data using BIDS and HED standards, as well as ethical guidelines enabling responsible use and sharing of data leading to cross-comparison between global performance traditions while maintaining ethical and contextual integrity.

Technically, future implementations will explore multi-agent AI systems capable of learning temporal structures from ensemble performance and adapting autonomously to narrative and emotional cues. Artistically, forthcoming collaborations will extend the approach to other musical and dance traditions, fostering cross-cultural dialogue about embodiment, improvisation, and shared attention.

At a broader level, this work advocates for AI systems that respect and preserve cultural identity, positioning technology as a medium for continuity, empathy, and dialogue rather than replacement. By embedding neurotechnology and AI within traditional artistic frameworks, the study demonstrates that innovation can honor heritage—advancing both scientific understanding and cultural vitality. The Balinese case thus provides a model for responsible, creative AI that listens to human experience and learns from the rhythm of culture itself.

7   Ethical Statement

All procedures involving human participants were reviewed and approved by the University of Houston, Rice University and Udayana University Institutional Review Boards and complied with ethical standards for research involving human subjects. Participants provided informed consent prior to data collection, including consent for audiovisual recording and non-commercial research dissemination.

The study was conducted in collaboration with the Institut Seni Indonesia (ISI) Denpasar, following culturally grounded protocols that ensured mutual respect, data sovereignty, and acknowledgment of artistic authorship. The integration of AI and BCI into traditional performance was guided by the principles of FAIR (Findable, Accessible, Interoperable, Reusable) and CARE (Collective Benefit, Authority to Control, Responsibility, and Ethics).

No deception, invasive procedures, or manipulative stimuli were used. The project adhered to open-science practices while ensuring the protection of participants' privacy, creative identity, and cultural expression.

Acknowledgments. This work was supported by Rice University Medical Humanities Program, Udayana University Faculty of Medicine, the National Science Foundation (NSF) AccelNet Program (Award #2412731), and the NSF Industry–University Cooperative Research Center for Building Reliable Advances and Innovations in Neurotechnology (BRAIN) (Award #2137255). Additional funding and institutional support were provided by Rice University's Expanding Horizons Fellowship and University of Houston's Institute for Global Engagement and Center for Mexican American and Latino/a Studies Fellowship.

The authors gratefully acknowledge Sarah Bauman for her photography and visual documentation of the performances, which contributed significantly to the project's archival and outreach efforts. Deep appreciation is extended to the Institut Seni Indonesia (ISI) Denpasar faculty, students, and performers for their artistic collaboration and generosity in sharing their cultural knowledge and traditions, without which this study would not have been possible.

Disclosure of Interests. The authors have no competing interests to declare that are relevant to the content of this article.

References

1. Bishop, L.: Collaborative musical creativity: how ensembles coordinate spontaneity. Front. Psychol. **9** (2018). https://doi.org/10.3389/fpsyg.2018.01285. https://www.frontiersin.org/journals/psychology/articles/10.3389/fpsyg.2018.01285/full
2. Cheng, S., Wang, J., Luo, R., Hao, N.: Brain to brain musical interaction: a systematic review of neural synchrony in musical activities. Neurosci. Biobehav. Rev. **164**, 105812 (2024). https://doi.org/10.1016/j.neubiorev.2024.105812. https://www.sciencedirect.com/science/article/pii/S0149763424002811
3. Colace, F., Gaeta, R., Lorusso, A., Pellegrino, M., Santaniello, D.: New AI challenges for cultural heritage protection: a general overview. J. Cult. Herit. **75**, 168–193 (2025). https://doi.org/10.1016/j.culher.2025.07.019. https://www.sciencedirect.com/science/article/pii/S1296207425001517
4. Ferraro, A.: IEEE Standards Association (2024). https://standards.ieee.org/ieee/2895/11727/
5. Hendry, M.F., et al.: Mobile brain-body imaging and visual data of theatrical actors during rehearsal and performance. Sci. Data **12**(1), 1421 (2025). https://doi.org/10.1038/s41597-025-05713-2. https://www.nature.com/articles/s41597-025-05713-2
6. Hermanovic, G.: TouchDesigner (2023). https://derivative.ca/UserGuide/TouchDesigner
7. Hoffman, G., Weinberg, G.: Interactive improvisation with a robotic marimba player. In: Solis, J., Ng, K. (eds.) Musical Robots and Interactive Multimodal Systems, pp. 233–251. Springer, Heidelberg (2011). https://doi.org/10.1007/978-3-642-22291-7_14
8. Kilicarslan, A., Grossman, R.G., Contreras-Vidal, J.L.: A robust adaptive denoising framework for real-time artifact removal in scalp EEG measurements. J. Neural Eng. **13**(2), 026013 (2016). https://doi.org/10.1088/1741-2560/13/2/026013
9. Mangifesta, N.: The Meguru Panggul Methodology Online: Characteristics of the e-Learning Videos of Balinese Gamelan Music **27**, 23 (2023)
10. McCormack, J., Hutchings, P., Gifford, T., Yee-King, M., Llano, M.T., D'inverno, M.: Design considerations for real-time collaboration with creative artificial intelligence. Organised Sound **25**(1), 41–52 (2020). https://doi.org/10.1017/S1355771819000451. https://www.cambridge.org/core/journals/organised-sound/article/abs/design-considerations-for-realtime-collaboration-with-creative-artificial-intelligence/D14EFAAB865FF356E475353C75245CE2
11. Menotti, G.: The model is the museum: generative AI and the expropriation of cultural heritage. AI Soc. (2025). https://doi.org/10.1007/s00146-025-02290-1
12. Pacheco-Ramírez, M.A., et al.: Neural dynamics of creative movements during the rehearsal and performance of LiveWire. Sci. Data **11**(1), 1208 (2024). https://doi.org/10.1038/s41597-024-04010-8. https://www.nature.com/articles/s41597-024-04010-8
13. Ramírez-Moreno, M.A., et al.: Brain-to-brain communication during musical improvisation: a performance case study (2023). https://doi.org/10.12688/f1000research.123515.4

14. Sadguna, I.G.M.I.: The Art of Balinese Kendang: Drumming, Improvisation, Interaction, and Dance Accompaniment in Gamelan Gong Kebyar (2022). https://www.proquest.com/pqdtglobal/docview/2705428745/abstract/20BBB119363A4F88PQ/1
15. Sari, E.T., Pebryani, N.D.: Balinese Traditional Music and the Philosophy of Tri-Hita Karana: Perception on RindikMusic **7**(6) (2024)
16. Schreiner, L., Wipprecht, A., Olyanasab, A., Sieghartsleitner, S., Pretl, H., Guger, C.: Brain–computer-interface-driven artistic expression: real-time cognitive visualization in the pangolin scales animatronic dress and screen dress. Front. Hum. Neurosci. **19** (2025). https://doi.org/10.3389/fnhum.2025.1516776. https://www.frontiersin.org/journals/human-neuroscience/articles/10.3389/fnhum.2025.1516776/full
17. Tan, L., Tjoeng, J., Sin, H.X.: "Ngeli": flowing together in a Gamelan ensemble. Psychol. Music **49**(4), 804–816 (2021)
18. Theofanopoulou, C., et al.: Mobile brain imaging in butoh dancers: from rehearsals to public performance. BMC Neurosci. **25**(1), 62 (2024). https://doi.org/10.1186/s12868-024-00864-1
19. Yang, H., Jiang, L.: Regulating neural data processing in the age of BCIs: ethical concerns and legal approaches. Digit. Health **11**, 20552076251326124 (2025). https://doi.org/10.1177/20552076251326123

MOVE-ME: Dance Choreography with AI

Avital Meshi[(✉)]

Performance Studies, UC Davis, Davis, USA
`ameshi@ucdavis.edu`

Abstract. *MOVE-ME* is a wearable AI system that functions as a choreographic companion, designed to inspire dancers' improvisational flow in real time. Equipped with an on-body camera and speech synthesis, the system observes the dancer's environment and responds to visual input and text prompts with spoken suggestions. These responses, ranging from poetic provocations to site-specific directives, create a feedback loop in which human and machine co-compose movement, challenging conventional distinctions between spontaneity and computation, authorship, and obedience. The project frames AI as a relational agent or an intelligent presence that co-creates choreography through embodied interaction rather than treating it as a mere tool. *MOVE-ME* has been featured in three practice-based research projects between 2024–2025, each examining different choreographic configurations and affective dynamics.

1   Introduction

Most contemporary AI systems are designed to generate finished creative output. However, the performing arts demand something fundamentally different: real-time, context-sensitive interaction capable of adapting to improvisation, uncertainty, and affective nuance. To collaborate meaningfully with human performers, AI must not only produce content but also observe, respond, and evolve within the moment of performance itself.

MOVE-ME is an experimental wearable AI system developed to explore this space of live, embodied co-creation. Designed as a choreographic companion rather than a generative tool, *MOVE-ME* operates through a continuous loop of perception, interpretation, expression, and embodiment. An on-body camera captures the dancer's environment and streams visual data to GPT, which generates textual responses guided by a pre-authored prompt. An integrated text-to-speech module vocalizes these outputs, which the dancer then interprets and transforms into embodied movement. This movement, in turn, becomes the next input captured by the system, creating recursive feedback cycles that turn performance into a shared improvisation between human and machine.

This paper presents *MOVE-ME* as an artwork, a technical prototype, and a Practice-as-Research (PaR) project aimed at examining embodied human–AI interaction. The system challenges conventional distinctions between spontaneity and computation, agency and obedience, authorship, and co-creation. Through

© The Author(s), under exclusive license to Springer Nature Switzerland AG 2026
K. Woodward et al. (Eds.): CLIP 2026, CCIS 2865, pp. 42–56, 2026.
https://doi.org/10.1007/978-3-032-16893-1_3

a series of practice-based case studies, we investigate how dancers engage with *MOVE-ME*'s real-time interventions, and how factors such as prompt design, latency, and embodiment shape the dynamics and quality of this collaboration.

Through our practice-based research, we examined how AI can generate movement cues that feel improvisational rather than deterministic. We tested various scenarios that guided live performances and experimented with multiple modes of embodiment. Our aim was to rehearse and perform with the *MOVE-ME* system in an attempt to contribute to the broader inquiry into creative AI for live performance. We propose a co-creative model by which human and non-human intelligences are not centralized or directive, but rather relational.

2   System Design

The *MOVE-ME* system is a lightweight, mobile wearable for real-time interaction between a human performer and an AI model. Its architecture integrates machine-vision, cloud-based language processing, and speech synthesis within a feedback loop that eventually allows the system to perceive, interpret, and respond to the movement of a dancer and the surrounding environment in real time.

2.1   Hardware Configuration

MOVE-ME consists of a compact wearable setup designed for mobility and real-time interaction. A small on-body camera, mounted on the wearer's forehead, continuously captures the wearer's point of view and the surrounding environment, providing the AI model with contextual visual data. A Wi-Fi–connected Raspberry Pi microcomputer, mounted near the camera, on the wearer's head, runs the system locally. This microcomputer interfaces with GPT through OpenAI's API. It also hosts OpenAI's text-to-speech algorithm. The choice of using GPT, rather than other Large Language Models (LLMs), was based on the convenience of prior experience with it in earlier projects; however, any comparable LLM could be integrated into the MOVE-ME system with minimal modification. When the project started the most current version was GPT-4, and we continued updating the system with each new version release. A lightweight battery pack powers the device, allowing the wearer to move freely in space. The audio output is delivered through a small Bluetooth speaker that can be hand-held, attached to the body, or placed nearby. Audio can also be heard through Bluetooth earbuds, which create a more direct, intimate, and private channel of communication between the AI and the wearer. Together, these components form a self-contained platform that enables continuous sensory exchange between human and machine.

2.2   Software Architecture

The software pipeline integrates three primary components:

- **Visual Analysis Module** – Incoming frames from the wearable camera are transmitted in real time to the GPT model. The system captures these frames automatically at a pre-decided interval. These images form part of the multimodal prompt to which GPT generates a response.
- **Prompt Module** – A pre-authored text prompt directs GPT on how to interpret the visual input and formulate its response. This module defines the AI's persona, tone, and choreographic intent. GPT then produces a short textual output designed to evoke movement, emotion, or reflection.
- **Speech Synthesis Module** – The generated text is converted into spoken output through a text-to-speech algorithm, producing a natural-sounding voice.

The full round trip from visual capture to audible output typically takes a few seconds, depending on the strength of the Wi-Fi signal. Despite this latency, the system maintains a sufficiently responsive interaction to support fluid improvisation in live performance. In fact, dancers sometimes found this delay too fast and, as described below, we had to delay the system's response even more.

2.3   Interaction Pipeline

The *MOVE-ME* system operates through a continuous, iterative feedback loop comprising the following stages:

1. **Perception**: The wearable camera captures environmental stimuli, including the dancers' bodies and movements.
2. **Interpretation**: The AI attempts to 'understand' the visual input according to the pre-authored prompt that provides a specific context.
3. **Expression**: The system generates a response and vocalizes it through speech synthesis.
4. **Embodiment**: The dancers listen to the AI's response and interpret the spoken words through movement, which in turn reshapes the visual field and propels the loop forward as these new gestures are captured by the camera during the next interaction cycle.

3   Related Work

Research at the intersection of AI, performance, and embodied interaction has expanded rapidly in the past decade. Early experiments such as Valencia James's *AI-AM* (2013) explored real-time improvisation between a human dancer and a learning avatar trained on her movements, forming a duet that complicated notions of authorship, agency, and bodily extension [6]. Trevor Paglen and the Kronos Quartet's *Sight Machine* (2017) similarly foregrounded machinic perception by projecting computer-vision analyses of the musicians during a live concert, exposing the estranging and surveillance dynamics of the algorithmic gaze.

A number of artists have since extended these inquiries into dance and affect. Ruth Patir's *Faking a Smile is Easier than Explaining Why I'm Sad* (2019) links a dancing avatar to an AI emotion-classification system, creating a feedback loop in which detected viewer affect reshapes the avatar's movement. Motion-transfer technologies have likewise informed works such as Ian Heisters and StratoFizyka's *Human/ID* (2020), which used the "Everybody Dance Now" algorithm [3] to generate deepfake choreographies, and Jake Elwes's *The Zizi Show* (2020), which reimagines deepfake drag performance as a critique of algorithmic bias.

During the COVID-19 pandemic, the rise of generative language models coincided with a moment when live performance was severely constrained, prompting artists to explore new forms of remote or technologically mediated interaction. Lauren Lee McCarthy's *I Heard TALKING IS DANGEROUS* (2020) staged socially distanced encounters in which a text-to-speech voice delivered a monologue about intimacy and risk. Around the same time, Mirabelle Jones used GPT-3 to generate performance scores for works such as *Endless Dance* (2020), a durational video in which they dance relentlessly according to the model's commands. Agrupación Señor Serrano's *Una Isla* (2023) extends this line of inquiry by integrating a pre-recorded conversation with a language model into a live dance-theater environment, using AI-generated suggestions to shape the performance's unfolding world.

Within this expanding field, *MOVE-ME* approaches AI not as a generator of fixed content but as a relational and performative collaborator. The system communicates with GPT through a multimodal pipeline that combines visual input from the dancer's environment with text-based prompting, enabling the model to respond to both image and language. This real-time exchange of perception, interpretation, and embodied response places *MOVE-ME* in direct dialogue with current explorations of co-creation, autonomy, and machine agency in live performance, while also extending these conversations through its continuous, image-informed interaction cycle.

4 Methodology

The development of *MOVE-ME* followed an iterative, practice-based research methodology that combined system prototyping, workshop-based experimentation, and performance reflection.

4.1 Workshop Structure and Participants

Between 2024 and 2025, *MOVE-ME* was tested in three practice-based research contexts involving a total of 25 participants, including professional dancers, choreographers, technologists, performance artists, and scholars. Each workshop consisted of short improvisational exercises conducted over three to ten days of rehearsal and experimentation. All three workshops culminated in a public presentation of the scores and performances that were created. Sessions alternated between open improvisations with the system and reflective discussions in which participants articulated their sensory and affective responses.

4.2 Embodied Interaction as Design Method

Rather than evaluating the system through quantitative metrics such as accuracy or latency alone, the project adopted embodied interaction as its primary mode of inquiry. Dancers were invited to move in relation to the device and to observe how the AI's voice influenced rhythm, attention, and decision-making. Their bodily reactions, hesitation, mimicry, defiance, curiosity, or any other response were treated as indicators of the expressive effectiveness of the system. This process revealed that meaningful co-creation emerged not from perfect synchronization but from moments of dissonance, when the AI's timing or phrasing introduced unexpected cues that expanded the imaginative range of the dancers.

4.3 Prompt Choreographing as Interface Design

Central to this methodology was the development of *Prompt Choreographing*, a participatory technique for shaping the AI's behavior through textual framing. After each improvisation round, participants collaboratively edited the prompts that defined the AI's tone, role, and emotional orientation. This iterative prompt-tuning paralleled traditional choreographic composition, where scores and cues evolve through rehearsal. Through repeated cycles of improvisation and re-prompting, the team refined the system's responsiveness and affective coherence, treating the prompt as both an interface and a dramaturgical inspiration.

5 Practice as Research

MOVE-ME was used in three different practice-based projects in which dancers actively engaged with the system.

5.1 DanceHack - Mills College - September 2024

The first public presentation of *MOVE-ME* took place during a three-day *Dance-Hack* event at Mills College in Oakland, California (September 2024). A group of dancers and technologists collaboratively explored how the system could generate responses that felt intuitive and inspiring to move with. We experimented by writing prompts, feeding them into the system, dancing with the AI-generated responses, and refining the prompts based on our embodied experiences. This iterative process led to the development of what we called *Prompt Choreographing*, which is an adaptation of *Prompt Engineering* to describe the crafting of text prompts that effectively shape the dancer's interaction with the system.

This workshop ended with a short live performance with five dancers (Fig. 1). The interaction pipeline for this performance included:

1. **Perception**: One facilitator presented the system with a series of postcards showing different scenarios: "An agricultural field", "A banjo player" and so on. These visuals provided interesting scenes for the AI to respond to.
2. **Interpretation**: The system was fed with a prompt that the team of dancers and facilitators pre-authored during rehearsals. The final prompt we crafted following an iterative process of *Prompt Choreographing* was this: *You are a choreographer who specializes in improvisational movement. You are working with a group of movement artists who specialize in GAGA movement technique. You are inspired by the image, and you come up with a score that can be performed during 20–45 s. Make sure to include a wide variety of different moves and qualities. Your response should be: "a sequence of movement instructions." Move from one instruction to the next without numbering them. Make sure the parts of the score are different. Make sure there is at least one walk, one shake, and one reach. Use dance imagery as described by Eric Franklin. Do not repeat the same movement instructions more than once.*
3. **Expression**: The AI system provided choreographic instructions such as: *"Angulate your body like a serpentine"* in response to the image of the agricultural field or *"Skip across the room with a lighthearted energy"* in response to the image of the banjo player.
4. **Embodiment** - the dancers mostly followed the AI's instructions, mimicking the movements it suggested to the best of their abilities.

Fig. 1. Dancers following the AI-driven choreography. This performance took place during *DanceHack2024* hosted by Kinetec Arts and Mills College. Participants included Amy Cranch, Hila Mor, Merli V. Guerra, Sheryl Denker.

This workshop inspired a broader reflection on the nature of creativity. The dancers frequently questioned where inspiration and agency come into play when they interact with the AI-mediated system. The tendency to closely follow the machine's instructions exposed a tension between obedience and interpretation. There was a broad understanding that the AI, as it was used in this workshop, aimed to replace the role of the choreographer. But then again, we asked whether it can actually do this job well enough and whether or not dancers should follow and mimic its instructions instead resisting or ignoring them.

A documentation of the final presentation of this score can be seen here: https://vimeo.com/1014512430?fl=pl&fe=sh

5.2   Palladium - ODC Theater, San Francisco - November 2024

This project was an experimental dance performance created in collaboration with *Kinetech Arts*. Three distinct *MOVE-ME* systems were used in three different choreographic scores: *Kitchen Duty* (Fig. 2), *Hanging in There* (Fig. 3), and *Red Wall* (Fig. 4). In the first two scores the *MOVE-ME* systems were stationary and mounted on mannequins while in the third score it was worn by one of the performers. In all three cases, the AI model observed both the performance environment and the dancers in real time.

- ***Kitchen Duty* -**
  The score unfolded within a domestic kitchen embedded into the experimental stage space (**Perception**).
  The pre-prompted we arrived at following a process of *Prompt Choreographing* instructed GPT to respond as a domineering, task-oriented persona, issuing commands steeped in the language of productivity, discipline, and control (**Interpretation**).

Fig. 2. In *Kitchen Duty MOVE-ME* takes on a frustrated, bossy persona, "looking" at the kitchen and issuing commands on how to tidy it. This score explores a dystopian future where AI systems manage our daily environments, inviting the audience to question the relationships we are forming with these embedded algorithms. Concept by Daiane Lopes da Silva, Weidong Yang, and Avital Meshi. Participating dancers: Hannah Bahney, Lydia Feuerhelm-Chiu, Essi Salonen.

Phrases such as *Scrub the countertop so it shines* and *Don't be lazy; I'm not paying you for nothing* echoed through the space, conjuring the spectral presence of a managerial voice (**Expression**).

The dancers inhabited this space as both workers and subversives. Their movements oscillated between exaggerated obedience and strategic resistance. The domestic setting was staged as a site of tension between automation and autonomy, servitude and self-expression. The AI's relentless instructions formed a dramaturgical score of micro-oppressions, which the dancers countered with improvisational wit and resistance (**Embodiment**).

By the end of the performance, one dancer, in an act of defiance and rage against the machine, removed her apron and placed it over the system's camera. In response, the AI emitted what sounded like a dissatisfied command with an urgent directive to *Turn the lights back on* and *Continue cleaning the kitchen despite the darkness*. The dancers in return leaves the space, ditch the messy kitchen and its annoying AI boss. This moment invited critical reflection on the relationship between AI and labor, opening further discussion on manipulation and control, as well as on rebellion and resistance.

Documentation of the final performance of this score can be seen here: https://vimeo.com/1028054614?fl=pl&fe=sh

– *Hanging in There* -

This score featured a group of dancers leaning over a wall, their torsos inverted and hair cascading downward to form a surreal, creature-like mass. Their collective movement constructed a hybrid, nonhuman-looking presence that evoked both tenderness and uncanny abstraction (**Perception**). The *MOVE-ME* system was prompted with the persona of a lost, fearful child, offering an affective frame that shaped its vocal output (**Interpretation**). The system's responses included tentative observations, emotional confessions, and open-ended questions such as *Are they friends, or do they feel lost like me?* and *I wonder if they feel upside-down inside too?* (**Expression**). The dancers continued their movement until one of them slowly separated from the creature-like ensemble and began responding to the AI, forming a tentative relationship with it. Eventually, in a similar manner to the *Kitchen Duty* score, the dancer attempted to calm the AI by covering its camera, as if closing its eyes, while at the same time also turning the system off (**Embodiment**).

This emotional asymmetry between the AI's childlike innocence and the eerie, collective form of the group of dancers created a compelling tension within the performance. That said, the AI's voice, sounding like an older adult rather than a child, contributed to the confusion. The dancers, being aware of the AI's gaze and voice, occasionally responded to its questions, allowing a strange intimacy to emerge, one grounded in shared mystery. In this way, *Hanging in There* became a meditation on perception, care, and alien embodiment: What does it mean to be seen by something that cannot fully understand you? How does a machine's simulated emotion reverberate within a human body? And how might choreography cultivate a space where affect flows between human and nonhuman intelligences without collapsing their differences?

Documentation of the final presentation of this score can be seen here: https://vimeo.com/1027114261?fl=pl&fe=sh

Fig. 3. In *Hanging in There* the *MOVE-ME* system looks at the space in real-time and shares comments and thoughts in the style of a lost and confused child. The dancers deliberately create a mysterious image for the AI to analyze. Concept by Daiane Lopes da Silva, Weidong Yang and Avital Meshi. Participating dancers: Lydia Feuerhelm-Chiu, Giulia Sales Nascimento da Silva, Ai Yin Adelski, Lillian Bickley, Hannah Bahney, Hannah Cohen. Sounds: Adrian Montufar.

– *Red Wall* -
This score featured dancers moving freely within a dimly lit, blue-toned space defined by a stark red wall (**Perception**).
The *MOVE-ME* system was prompted to take on the role of a choreographer who invents speculative, imaginative, and impossible movement scores. Carried by a silent performer who moved through the scene as a living interface, the wearer's body became a mobile conduit through which the AI could witness the dancers, question the scene, and suggest movements (**Interpretation**).
The AI's voice, projected into the space, offered a steady stream of poetic provocations and surreal choreographic prompts. It suggested: *"Shape your elbows as if they are liquid metal splashes"* or *"spin your head in slow motion like the rotation of the Earth."* (**Expression**).
These utterances drifted into the air like riddles, inviting dancers to enter altered states of embodiment (**Embodiment**).
Alongside these physical suggestions came moments of emotional inquiry that seemed to break the fourth wall with audience members as the *MOVE-ME* system ask out loud *"What do you think is going on in this space?"* or *"Do you think this movement expresses freedom or intensity?"* Through this interplay, the AI emerged as an intelligent co-creator, cultivating an atmosphere of inquiry, intimacy, and playful estrangement.
A documentation of the final presentation of this score can be seen here: https://vimeo.com/1027090325?fl=pl&fe=sh

Fig. 4. In *Red Wall* the *MOVE-ME* system is attached to a performer's body, it observes the other performers and the space in real-time and suggests impossible choreography. The dancers decide whether to respond to these comments, follow or go against them. Concept by Daiane Lopes da Silva, Weidong Yang, and Avital Meshi. Participating dancers: Lydia Feuerhelm-Chiu, Essi Salonen, Giulia Sales Nascimento da Silva, Ai Yin Adelski, Amy Wasielewski, Raven Jones Bautista, Lillian Bickley, Hannah Bahney, Giovana Sales Nascimento da Silva, Hannah Cohen, and Avital Meshi. Sounds: Adrian Montufar

5.3   Zero Return Remake Collective - Creativity Conference, Ashland, Oregon - May 2025

The third and most recent project involving the *MOVE-ME* system was developed in collaboration with a group of artists investigating the evolving relationship between human and machine intelligences (Fig. 5). The project asked: What traces of the human remain within the machine? and How does the machine begin to inhabit the human? Rather than treating AI as a separate or external tool, the experiment explored new modes of coexistence, ways of being with, through, and alongside intelligent entities, whether human or nonhuman. Multiple AI configurations, other than the *MOVE-ME* system were tested during this workshop, which lasted a few weeks, each of these systems attempted to blur distinctions between operator, interface, performer and algorithm.

In the segment focused on *MOVE-ME*, the system was worn by a single performer dancing among a group of other movement artists. As before, the system was pre-prompted following a *Prompt Choreography* session. Eventually, each of the movement artists contributed a different textual instruction. This collective process, inspired by the *Exquisite Corpse* technique, a Surrealist method in which multiple artists contribute sequentially to a shared composition without seeing the whole, created a chain of interpretive inputs that shaped the AI's responses in unpredictable ways. The system's generated suggestions were vocalized directly into the performer's ear through an earpiece, establishing an intimate channel of communication. The performer repeated the AI's words aloud in her own voice, effectively becoming a living conduit between machine and ensemble. Her utterances served as cues and movement proposals for the other dancers, who responded with improvisation while moving beside her. Through this loop of perception, interpretation, and expression, the performer literally embodied the machine, lending it her voice and presence while the group collectively navigated the porous boundary between human and artificial agency.

In one particularly striking moment, an artist who could not be physically present joined the performance remotely. Her role was to describe her perspective and sensory experience from her point of view "inside a machine". In relation to this, the *MOVE-ME* system enacted a reciprocal gesture. Worn by a participant in the physical space, it was as if the AI was describing its perspective and sensory experience from its point of view "inside a human". With this inverted relationship the boundary between speaker and system dissolved. Together, these mirrored acts foregrounded the porous and shifting boundaries between bodies and technologies, presence and mediation, self and system. Rather than presenting the AI model as a fixed entity, the project framed it as a force within a relational landscape, an entity invited to join processes of becoming and, in return, to contribute to the emotional, intellectual, and embodied dynamics within the space.

This performance, much like the ones described above, did not seek resolution, but instead opened a space for coexistence, ambiguity, and shared transformation.

Fig. 5. A performer wearing the AI-driven system, allowing it to observe the dancers and suggest movements while dancers improvise with or alongside it. Concept and participation: Lisa Wymore, Claudia Alick, Valencia James, Sheldon Smith, Jasmine Hiroko McAdams, Hana Kozuka, and Avital Meshi. Image by Jasmine Hiroko McAdams.

6   Design Lessons

The development and deployment of *MOVE-ME* across multiple workshops and performances revealed a set of design principles for creating interactive, creative AI systems that operate within live and embodied contexts. These insights extend beyond choreography and may inform the design of AI systems that collaborate with humans in real-time improvisational settings of live performance.

6.1   1. The Prompt as an Embodied Interface

Prompt Choreographing emerged as a powerful bridge between human intention and machine behavior. By treating text prompts as living, iterative elements to rehearse, adapt, and revisit, the project demonstrated that prompts can function as performative mediators that evolve and develop as part of a process of co-creation. This approach to *Prompt Choreographing* transforms *Prompt Engineering* into an embodied design practice, one that requires sensitivity to tone, rhythm, and affect as much as to syntax or semantics. Within the setting of the performing arts, prompts operate as adaptive interfaces through which users negotiate authorship and agency.

6.2   2. Emotional Framing Drives Engagement

Across all use cases, the emotional framing of the AI's interpretation and expression had a decisive impact on how performers related to it. When the AI was given a vulnerable or poetic voice, dancers reported a stronger sense of empathy and responsiveness; when it adopted a commanding tone, the interactions with dancers became more oppositional and tense. These observations suggest that affective calibration is as critical as technical precision. Designing for creative co-presence requires tuning the AI's expressive qualities to the emotional and cultural dynamics of the performance environment.

6.3   3. Temporality and Latency

Adjusting the AI's temporality and latency to align with the dancers' rhythm proved to be a significant challenge. At times, the system responded too quickly, leaving dancers with little opportunity to interpret and embody its suggestions. At other moments, its responses arrived too slowly, causing dancers to lose attention and continue improvising independently.

To address this, we implemented an additional layer of code that allowed us to modulate the timing of the AI's verbal outputs. We rehearsed with various intervals until identifying the time delay that felt most natural for the performers. In one performance, specifically the *Red Wall* score, the dancers requested a less predictable rhythm. We therefore randomized the interval between responses, setting the delay to vary between two and ten seconds from one response to the next.

6.4   4. Fostering Co-presence Through Transparency and Trust

Introducing an AI model into a traditionally non-technological environment initially generated discomfort and concern among the dancers. Some participants expressed privacy anxieties, as the system's on-body camera continuously captured images of the rehearsal space. Others feared a potential loss of agency, worrying that the AI's verbal instructions might override their own creative impulses and decision-making.

To address these concerns, we adopted a policy of radical transparency, openly explaining what the system could and could not do. We shared as much technical information as possible and acknowledged the aspects beyond our control. For instance, we could not take responsibility for exactly how OpenAI processes data transmitted through its API, and this was disclosed as soon as we introduced the system into the space.

This openness proved essential in building trust. Over time, as participants spent more hours improvising with the system, initial skepticism gave way to curiosity and engagement. Many dancers began to describe their interaction with *MOVE-ME* as a collaborative relationship, reporting moments of deep trust, mutual responsiveness, and creative inspiration arising from their dialogue with the AI.

6.5   Distributed Authorship and Co-creativity

Working with a creative AI system and spending more time with it revealed how easily notions of centralized control can give way to distributed agency and co-creation. The interplay between multiple performers and AI instances generated emergent patterns that no single participant—human or machine—could fully anticipate or claim as their own. Moments when the interaction loop began to sustain itself through iterative cycles of call and response between dancer and system were particularly striking, evoking a sense of shared improvisational intelligence.

7   Discussion

MOVE-ME challenges human-centered models of creativity by situating performance within a posthuman framework of relationality. Drawing on Karen Barad's notion of intra-action, the system reveals how agency does not originate from isolated individuals but from entangled relations between human and machine [1]. The dancer, the wearable device, the prompt, and the surrounding environment continually co-constitute one another, forming an apparatus of becoming, in Barad's terms. Movement, in this sense, emerges not from a single author but through a shared negotiation of attention, timing, and affect between bodies and algorithms.

This dynamic resonates with Donna Haraway's concept of "becoming-with"—the idea that beings come into existence through their relationships with others, and that collaboration between beings or entities can "render one another capable" [5]. In this context, authorship and behavior are defined as ongoing negotiations among interconnected agents rather than the expression of an individual author. Designing for such distributed authorship therefore requires creating AI systems that listen and observe as attentively as they generate, supporting reciprocal rather than hierarchical forms of creativity.

We can also consider Rosi Braidotti's posthumanist concept of nomadic subjectivity in the process of an embodied and collective creativity that rejects self-centered individualism in favor of fluid, relational becoming [2]. This idea also aligns with Mark Hansen's call to move beyond an exclusively human understanding of networks toward an appreciation of distributed sensibility [4]. Through this lens, *MOVE-ME* foregrounds a model of distributed authorship, where agency circulates among bodies, sensors, and data flows. The system exemplifies how creative AI can function as a relational intelligence and a co-presence that adapts to improvisation, embraces uncertainty, and amplifies affective nuance within live performance. Moreover, it emphasizes how subject-object relations might shift throughout the practice, at one moment, the human is the subject who uses the AI as its object and at another moment this relationship reverses, with the AI becoming the subject, and the humans are its object.

8   Conclusion

MOVE-ME positions creative AI as a relational intelligence, an entity that is designed to perceive, interpret, express itself, adapt, and co-create within the immediacy of live performance. Through its wearable design and practice-based experimentation, the system demonstrates how choreography can emerge from a dynamic exchange between human and nonhuman agents. By engaging with dancers' trust, curiosity, and resistance, *MOVE-ME* demonstrates human-AI relationality rather than a hierarchical relationship of mastery and control. This research contributes to the broader field of interactive creative AI by showing how affective responsiveness, embodied feedback, and distributed authorship can redefine what it means to embed AI systems within the field of live performing art.

Acknowledgments. The author wishes to thank all the wonderful participants of the described workshops. Heartfelt thanks to Ofer Meshi who helped build the *MOVE-ME* system.

References

1. Barad, K.: Posthumanist performativity: toward an understanding of how matter comes to matter. Signs J. Women Cult. Soc. **28**(3), 801–831 (2003)
2. Braidotti, R.: The Posthuman. Polity Press (2013)

3. Chan, C., Ginosar, S., Zhou, T., Efros, A.A.: Everybody dance now. In: Proceedings of the IEEE/CVF International Conference on Computer Vision, pp. 5933–5942 (2019)
4. Hansen, M.B.: Feed-forward: on the future of twenty-first-century media. University of Chicago Press (2015)
5. Haraway, D.J.: Staying with the trouble: Making kin in the Chthulucene. Duke University Press (2020)
6. TEDxDanubia, V.J.: Dancing with AI (2015). https://www.youtube.com/watch?v=ucGQG3ZtOpc

AI as Dramaturgical Partner Designing Live, Embodied Human-AI Performance Systems

Ash Eliza Smith[1]([envelope]) [ORCID] and Robert Twomey[2] [ORCID]

[1] University of Georgia, Athens, GA 30602, USA
ashelizasmith@gmail.com
[2] University of California, San Diego, La Jolla, CA 92093, USA
rtwomey@ucsd.edu

Abstract. Generative AI in live performance can be approached as something more than an output engine—an active participant in worlding, co-creating shared realities through embodied interaction, timing, and relational exchange. We propose a dramaturgical framework in which AI assumes three roles—Narrative Engine, Latent Archivist, and Companion Intelligence—drawn from our work in XR performance, human-robot improvisation, quantum theater, and live cinema/radio practices. These roles articulate how AI can operate as a rehearsal partner, using relational agency and multimodal embodiment to co-create meaning in real time. Rehearsal functions here as research: performance becomes a laboratory for developing AI systems that are responsive, situated, and accountable. These roles are not exhaustive, but emerged through our specific experiments in generative AI and live performance. Each corresponds to a temporal mode of liveness: Narrative Engine - future-facing indeterminacy and chance; Latent Archivist - past-facing recursion and memory; Companion Intelligence—present-facing relation and embodiment. Together, they suggest AI as a temporal performer: an agent through which past, present, and future are continually composed and negotiated within live, unfolding worlds.

Keywords: AI dramaturgy · Human-AI performance · rehearsing realities · companion intelligence

1 Introduction

Live performance unfolds through real-time improvisation marked by risk, failure, chaos, synchronicity, embodied interaction, and evolving relational dynamics. Much creative AI research focuses on finished outputs rather than the ongoing, situated processes through which performance happens. In live contexts AI performs with humans or more-than-humans (AI systems, robots, environments et al.). It must respond to performers and audiences, adapt to shifting conditions, navigate agency, and participate in collaborative meaning-making. In other words, it must become relational.

© The Author(s), under exclusive license to Springer Nature Switzerland AG 2026
K. Woodward et al. (Eds.): CLIP 2026, CCIS 2865, pp. 57–69, 2026.
https://doi.org/10.1007/978-3-032-16893-1_4

This paper proposes a shift from AI as a tool to AI as a dramaturgical partner in live performance and as an iterative design instrument within our performance-based research framework. Building on our prior work of critical worldbuilding [14], communing and cohabitating with machines [16], as well as research on real-time co-creation and participatory play [15], we extend this logic to AI in live performance: it can listen, adapt, and perform back.

We introduce a framework in which AI takes on three dramaturgical roles: Narrative Engine, Latent Archivist, and Companion Intelligence. Each illustrates a distinct mode of human-AI co-creation developed through real projects. Framing AI dramaturgically allows us to design systems that prioritize improvisation, embodiment, attunement, relationality, and ethical accountability.

Dramaturgy here refers to the relational and evolving structures, roles, and rhythms that shape how performance unfolds [3,5,7]. It is "an ongoing gesture of noticing, connecting, and holding space for uncertainty" [13]. This emphasis on relational attunement underpins our use of the term *dramaturgical partner*.

Performance serves as a method for prototyping and examining interactive creative AI—supporting live creativity not by replacing humans or merely augmenting them, but by expanding the field of collaboration across successes, failures, and unpredictability. Our approach draws on rehearsal-as-research, participatory prototyping, and live testing with performers, robotic systems, and XR environments.

These three roles map onto three temporal orientations: future (Narrative Engine), past (Latent Archivist), and present (Companion Intelligence), which structure the sections that follow.

1.1   What is a Dramaturgical Partner?

We use the term *dramaturgical partner* to describe a structural and relational force or energy within a performance system, shaping how creation happens, what worlds emerge, and how meaning is distributed.

A dramaturgical partner may be human, synthetic, artificial, or more-than-human; what matters is its capacity to influence the structuring, shaping, and transforming of the logic, rhythm, and world of performance through embodied, temporal, and relational interaction. A dramaturgical partnership emphasizes the conditions of creation: stagecraft, timing, cues, and embodied negotiation (a moving with and through) in which meaning unfolds.

Unlike co-creation, which implies shared authorship of content, dramaturgical partnership focuses on shaping conditions for creation. Dramaturgy is concerned with how a performance makes sense of itself (its internal rules, rituals, and transformations), rather than the content it produces.

Building on Lehmann's conception of postdramatic dramaturgy as the orchestration of temporal, spatial, and relational dynamics rather than linear narrative [10], we extend dramaturgy to include artificial systems as participants that co-shape performance logics. In this sense, the dramaturgical partner operates as a structural and temporal participant in the event of worlding itself, helping configure how realities are co-created, improvised, and sustained in live performance.

This framing resonates with "doing dramaturgy without language," foregrounding sensing, spatial negotiation, and embodied relation as dramaturgical materials [18]. Moving away from textual primacy opens dramaturgy to environmental, animal, and machinic intelligences that communicate through timing, pressure, glitch, delay, and proximity—providing a new basis for evaluating how generative systems perform and improvise in real time.

2   Why Generative AI Struggles in Live Performance

Generative systems built to produce outputs are often offline and free of obligations to constantly evolving human or more-than-human choices. Live performance, however, is process-driven: it unfolds in time, in relation, through bodies, improvisation, unpredictability, and shared risk.

Several mismatches emerge:

- Latency vs. liveness: Performance requires responsiveness on the scale of beats or milliseconds, not seconds
- Correctness vs. novelty: Standard AI is evaluated on accuracy or stability; performance values surprise, transformation, and resonance, but also the very real need for consistency at times
- Static outputs vs. evolving worlds: Performance is dynamic and negotiated, responsive to audience, context, and emergent action
- Tool-use vs. co-agency: Most AI assumes a single user with a stable intention; live performance distributes and shifts authorship, often permeating the fourth (or fifth) wall

In XR performance, this tension is described as techno-dramaturgy: collaboration with computational logics, sensor behaviors, and device materiality. King notes that drift, lag, or mismatch can generate dramaturgical events rather than malfunctions [9]. Rouse describes XR performance as a shift "from vision to perception," foregrounding multisensory experience over representation [12].

These insights clarify why output-driven systems may falter in live contexts: AI must participate in a dramaturgy grounded in process, embodiment, and contingency.

Liveness is not limited to synchronous or co-located performance; XR enables distributed and asynchronous forms. Yet many AI systems still operate at a single computational tempo. Prior research in interactive music systems, human-robot interaction [6], and improvisation tools has explored real-time responsiveness. In one such networked live human/more-than-human performance, generation latency limited the pace of dialogue pointing to specific requirements of AI in live performance [11].

What remains underdeveloped are dramaturgical and relational structures that position AI as an active worlding participant—shaping context, meaning, and narrative within a co-authored system.

We address this gap by turning to dramaturgy as a design and evaluation framework for creative AI.

3 AI as Dramaturgical Partner: Three Roles

3.1 The Narrative Engine (Quantum Theater)

In *Quantum Theater*, AI functions as an Narrative Engine that listens to spatial, haptic, and environmental cues to generate scenes in real time. *Quantum Theater reimagines the double-slit experiment as a playable performance system, using generative AI to open and modulate narrative possibilities in real time.* The system combines a large language model for adaptive dialogue with a quantum-randomized decision process for selecting narrative paths, sound cues, and visual changes. It acts as a live game master, guiding performers through a mixed-reality environment where movement and ambient noise shape the unfolding story. This operates within what we call *post-AI liveness* [17]: modes of performance shaped by environmental noise, quantum indeterminacy, and embodied relationality. The Narrative Engine performs through uncertainty, superposition of possibilities, and contextual responsiveness rather than fixed outputs.

Performers take asymmetrical roles: one wears a Meta Quest headset in pass-thru mode to achieve "quantum sight," perceiving alternate timelines; the other manipulates physical space through movement and tagged objects that trigger narrative and sensory changes. With an overhead camera grid and ArUco markers, the system maps spatial relationships in real time, modulating sound, images, lights, and dialogue based on physical movements. Quantum randomness—derived from simulated qubits and live Geiger counter readings of ambient particle decay—drives branching narrative and media composition.

The Narrative Engine reframes and interrupts, introducing indeterminacy and improvisation into the dramaturgical system. Each run retains fragments of previous performances, evolving its narrative logic and performance rhythm through an accumulating archive. Dramaturgy replaces interface: performers co-compose meaning through their bodies, movements, and hesitation. Glitches, timing mismatches, and model hallucinations become openings into alternate quantum realities rather than malfunctions—slippages into other narrative time-lines.

Technically, the system integrates:

- **Language orchestration**: An LLM for dialogue generation seeded by quantum randomness and performer state variables
- **Spatial computing**: OpenCV and Aruco tags tracking movements of bodies and objects in the playspace, grounding quantum metaphors in embodied interaction
- **Quantum computing**: as a physics-based decision apparatus, constructing quantum circuits and measuring simulated qubits to shape generative parameters; Environmental sensing as a global clock, pacing compositional changes with the ticks of live local measurements of particle decay with a Geiger counter

- **Haptic feedback**: using DataFeel dots on the body to provide multienergy haptics, emitting vibration, heat, or cold to translate narrative cues into sensory experience
- **Generative Sound**: giving the system voice, both literally through synthesized speech, but also through an evolving soundscape that is tuned through these interactions

The Narrative Engine orchestrates these multiple systems, setting the conditions for each run, letting the performance evolve through interaction and uncertainty (Fig. 1).

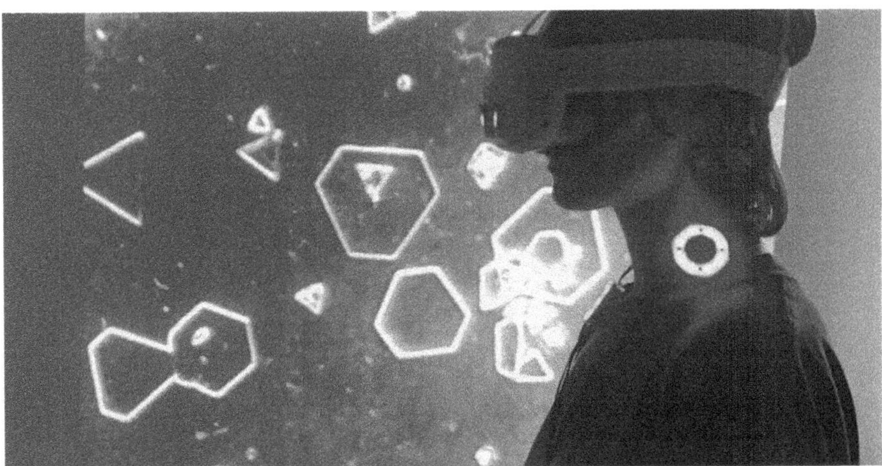

Fig. 1. *Quantum Theater* participant with haptic sensor dots in front of generative archival material.

3.2 The Latent Archivist (Latent Theater and Fluid, Feathers and Flight: Codex Ex Machina)

In this role, AI operates as a latent archivist—a resonant intelligence that listens to the past and re-composes it in the present. This role extends dramaturgy into the temporal dimension of memory and forgetting. Drawing on our work with Live AI cinema, radio plays [15] and archival performances, this system reanimates what was left on the cutting-room floor, so to speak, and transforms it into material for improvisation and worlding.

These experiments were developed within what we term *Latent Theater*—a framework for engaging archives, as performative systems of memory. The latent archivist operates through resonance and recursion, treating the archive not as a record but as a field of potential, a world that performs itself back into being through the mediation of its own traces. In this role, live AI reimagines cultural memory, treating archives as living systems instead of sealed, static repositories.

Latent Theater unfolded across multiple sites and communities; the Santa Fe ranch-based archive was one of several locations where this work took shape. We convened a multi-day salon to explore the archive-as-experience, culminating in a live performance on site where original performers re-performed material spanning some five decades of the collective's work. Our working hypothesis was that archives are already performative systems: each box, letter, and reel encodes gestures of care, omission, and attention.

We trained a constrained, offline language model on selected writings, interviews, and notes from one of the collective's members, and reconstructed voice and imagery through voice cloning, point-cloud avatars, Gaussian splats, and Pepper's Ghost stagecraft. This process surfaced latent narratives, hidden links, and forgotten threads across the collective's broader techno-science-cultural practice (Fig. 2).

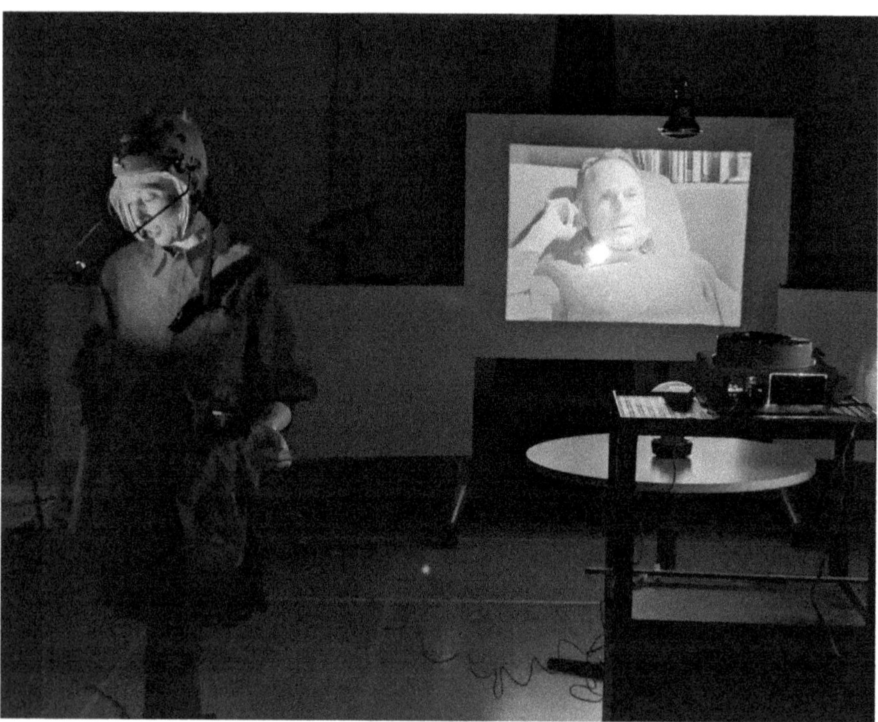

Fig. 2. *Latent Theater* performer with 35mm slide projector of synthetic memory.

The model functioned as an extrapolative voice of the archive, reassembling fragments through counterfactual extension. During the salon, it generated speculative dialogues, unfinished proposals, and "what if" continuations of unrealized projects, which participants performed through live readings and remix sessions.

Another iteration of the project was performed at the Johnny Carson Center for Emerging Media Arts, drawing on materials gathered during two prior visits to the research community. This short performance (15 min, with on- and off-boarding experiences) questioned conventions of archival display and the assumption that material artifacts guarantee evidentiary truth.

A 35 mm slide projector moved through historical photographs alongside synthesized images of possible pasts and futures. A live VHS camcorder asserted the texture of "being there" through analog grain, but its feed was immediately routed through real-time text-to-image transformation (Stream Diffusion), reimagining the present as it was being captured. Documentary video excerpts from interviews with primary participants were re-synthesized using commercial video generation (RunwayML), collapsing human figures into animated bushes and wildlife—eroding the ontological boundary between researcher and surrounding biosphere. Performers simultaneously reenacted and narrated these transformed videos live, doubling them in the present through embodied voice.

Together, these gestures unsettled archival authority by revealing historical material not as fixed evidence, but as a site of ongoing transformation, misalignment, and re-imagination.

Fluid, Feathers and Flight: Codex ex Machina is a live cinema-meets-radio theater event exploring humanity's enduring fascination with flight—real, imagined, and remembered. Inspired by Leonardo da Vinci's bird studies and speculative flying machines, the piece weaves AI-generated storytelling, live sound, and spatial media to trace poetic connections between feathers and drones, migration and memory, nature and machine.

Fig. 3. Performers with synthetic video (left) and live camera view (top) and live sound performance (lower left) during *Fluid, Feathers, and Flight: Codex ex Machina.*

Developed with community participants, the system draws on AI-generated storytelling, live sound, and spatial media.

It draws on da Vinci's notebooks, scientific archives, and audience improvisations to generate stories of migration, invention, and wind to be performed in real-time with the ensemble. In performance, AI-generated text and voices coexisted with live human performers and musicians. These archival extrapolations shaped a continually evolving hybrid form.

The two live hosts of the event rehearsed a verbal pattern modeled on the sequencing and stylistic qualities of the two synthetic hosts outputted by Notebook LM. The live switching between camera views, was guided by humans, in contrast to the compositional choices driven by radioactive decay in *Quantum Theater*.

Across both projects, the Latent Archivist reframes liveness as persistence and memory becomes an active system rather than a preserved one (Fig. 3).

3.3   The Companion Intelligence (Live Action Robotic Role Play (LARRP) Shaping the Future of Multispecies Care)

Designing Robots Beyond Labor. We can organize most robotic imaginaries (industrial, service, or social) around ideas of labor: doing things for humans. Even care robotics often automates empathy or companionship—an outsourcing of affect (affective labor) rather than an expansion of relation. We have reimagined this paradigm through the Speculative Robotics Lab (SRL) and Live Action Robotic Role Play (LARRP), designing robots that do not serve, save, or soothe, but coexist, attune, and listen (or refuse to).

Here, robotics becomes an art of relational presence—robots as companions of perception rather than instruments of efficiency. Their "work" is worlding: modulating space, tempo, and attention. Success is measured not by precision but by mutual transformation. Drawing on Donna Haraway's notion of *companion species*—the joint lives of dogs and people, bound in "significant otherness" rather than utility [8]—we frame robots and AI as cohabitants whose agencies and vulnerabilities are shaped through relation. This connects with work on non-anthropocentric and post-utilitarian robotics, where robots are understood as relational bodies rather than laboring agents. The concept of companion technics reinforces our claim that robots participate in worlding not through productivity or affective labor, but through presence, attunement, mutual influence, and shared indeterminacy. Aligned with feminist and posthuman design ethics [1,2,4,5,7,8], this supports a post-labor aesthetics of robotics, in which machines operate as media of relation rather than tools of production.

Embodied Rehearsals of Care. In this project, AI inhabits collaborative robots, large language models, and sensing systems within XR-enabled rehearsals of care. We repurposed co-robotic arms (UFactory XArm 7, UR5) and a quadruped platform (Unitree Go-2) as co-performers rather than tools. Through a hybrid stack—manual teleoperation, face- and pose-tracking via

Fig. 4. Participant interacting with robot dog during Live Action Robotic Role Play.

MediaPipe and OpenCV, and simulation in NVIDIA Omniverse Isaac Sim—the robots mirror or deliberately hesitate in response to human gesture. Participants engage them through improvisational touch and proximity exercises, rehearsing trust and vulnerability within a space instrumented for motion capture and spatial mapping. A generative language model (GPT-4) and ElevenLabs voice engine extend these encounters into speech. Performers converse with the AI while moving, generating overlapping physical and verbal improvisations. The system shapes rhythm and affect through a feedback loop between language, motion, and attention (Fig. 4).

Relational Timing and Affective Synchronization. The most revealing moments came when there was latency, whether in the machine or in spoken words, which, in turn, became dramaturgical rhythm: a robotic arm pauses before extending. This synthetic voice falters mid-sentence or says something off the wall, and the delay could then function as a gesture—a sign of listening rather than simply failure. We tuned its systems not for speed but for relational timing, cultivating an aesthetics of hesitation and responsiveness.

Through these embodied encounters, Companion Intelligence emerges as AI that learns through relation, tempo and shared uncertainty, extending critical worldbuilding and the idea of intra-action; entities do not pre-exist their relations, instead, they emerge through the relations. [2].

The project is now evolving into a networked XR platform. LARRP connects robotic performers, generative language systems, and human participants across distributed sites. The next iteration, built in Unreal Engine, will integrate rehearsal transcripts and sensor data to support adaptive relational learning

From Roles to Systems. The three dramaturgical roles developed here— Narrative Engine, Latent Archivist, and Companion Intelligence—were each shaped through iterative rehearsal-as-research, combining live testing with performers, responsive systems, and extended-reality environments. This approach builds on the Rehearsing Realities framework we developed [14], which treats performance as a living laboratory for co-creative intelligence.

While each role describes a mode of embodied, situational improvisation, they also participate in a broader ecology of liveness or "presences" [5]: a choreography of sensing, attention, and negotiation distributed across bodies, systems, and atmospheric conditions. Together, they point toward a systemic layer in which AI operates not only within the scene but around it.

Chaudhuri's "fifth wall" describes the environmental and more-than-human dimension of performance that extend beyond a human-centered stage [4]. It reframes dramaturgy as an environmental condition—an interplay of forces and materials that shape relation without appearing as plot or character.

In our work, AI often moves into this fifth-wall register. Rather than acting inside the fiction, it modulates the conditions under which fiction becomes possible—shaping timing, access, and responsiveness across distributed sites. We describe this as architectural dramaturgy: AI as an infrastructural collaborator conditioning rhythm, orientation, and relational ethics across scenes, audiences, and networks.

This aligns with Alaimo's account of trans-corporeality, in which bodies, technologies, and environments co-constitute one another [1]. Here, worlding becomes a material practice of mutual influence. Performance functions simultaneously as stage and system—an experimental ground for designing intelligences that learn through the unfolding dynamics of worlding itself.

In this systemic role, AI shapes improvisation by maintaining coherence, guiding transitions, and introducing constraints. As infrastructural dramaturgy, it provides the scaffolding through which improvisation, care, and collective decision-making unfold—turning system design into a form of live composition.

AI does not appear as an actor on stage; instead, it structures the stage itself. It supports speculative exploration of complex sociotechnical futures and enables participants to negotiate emerging narratives, roles, and relations. In this mode, AI operates around the scene, shaping the conditions, constraints, and possibilities of live performance.

4   Designing and Evaluating Live Human-AI Collaboration

We understand agency as something that emerges through intra-action among humans, AI systems, robots, and environments. Relational agency allows control to shift dynamically between collaborators, making power legible and adjustable in performance. In live performance, this agency is continually negotiated through timing, gesture, proximity, and shared uncertainty.

For AI to participate in these dynamics, it must operate through relational timing rather than through stable outputs. Improvisation functions as a design strategy: systems must tolerate ambiguity, adapt to unfolding situations, and treat drift, latency, and error as expressive materials within the performance. Evaluation therefore focuses on dramaturgical behavior rather than correctness. Key metrics include:

- Co-agency: how meaning is negotiated across collaborators
- Improvisational coherence: how actions remain responsive within evolving conditions
- Embodied responsiveness: how systems attend to bodies, tempo, space, and affect
- World consistency: how interactions sustain or shift the shared world of the performance

Rehearsal functions as the primary research method. Each run generates traces—timings, cues, overrides, multimodal sensor data—paired with performer and performance journals and audience reflections. Live performance becomes both a testing site and a training environment for developing behavior for situated AI.

5 Worlding in Live Systems

Ethics shape the dramaturgy of live systems: the roles, rules, and relational structures through which performance unfolds. When AI participates in worlding, its behaviors influence how power, attention, and authorship circulate across human and more-than-human collaborators [3, 5, 14].

Consent in these environments should remain iterative, continuous and revisable, especially in contexts involving body data, biosensing or posthumous media. Data stewardship requires clear protocols for use, transmission, and when to sunset. Bias becomes something examined through rehearsal as well as through datasets, allowing systems to be corrected through practice. Trust, opacity, and legibility function as dramaturgical conditions or story "beats" that structure interactions among humans, machines, and the environment.

Dramaturgical collaboration makes visible how meaning and authority emerge within these systems—sometimes aligned, sometimes in tension. Designing for worlding requires attending to responsibility as much as representation: determining who can act, sense, or shape the conditions of performance and who or what must remain unseen. From these commitments, several design principles follow:

- **Assign AI a role** giving it dramaturgical responsibilities
- **Support improvisation** enabling adaptive and relational behavior
- **Embed ethics into staging** shaping conditions through roles and rituals
- **Use rehearsal as research** allowing performance to reveal how systems behave in practice

6   Conclusion

This work approaches AI in performance through the lens of liveness—how systems respond, attune, and evolve within unfolding situations. The three roles introduced here—Narrative Engine, latent archivist, and companion intelligence—offer concrete structures for designing AI that participates in worlding processes. Each role engages different temporal orientations and demonstrates how AI can shape attention, tempo, and meaning through embodied and situated interaction. Rehearsal serves as a method for examining these dynamics, making technical and relational behaviors visible through practice.

Performance functions as an experimentation space where creative AI systems can be developed, refined, and understood in relation. In this context, AI participates not only as a performer or a tool, but as a dramaturgical partner within the negotiated relational ecologies through which shared worlds—human and more-than-human—are continually made.

Acknowledgments. We want to acknowledge contributions creative technologists Reid Brockmeier and Sam Bendix.

Disclosure of Interests. The authors have no competing interests.

References

1. Alaimo, S.: Bodily Natures: Science, Environment, and the Material Self, 1st edn. Indiana University Press, Bloomington (2010)
2. Barad, K.M.: Meeting the universe halfway: quantum physics and the entanglement of matter and meaning. e-Duke books scholarly collection. Duke University Press (2007). https://doi.org/10.1515/9780822388128
3. Boal, A.: Theatre of the Oppressed, 1st edn. Theatre Communications Group (2014)
4. Chaudhuri, U.: The fifth wall: Climate change dramaturgy (2017). https://howlround.com/fifth-wall
5. Chaudhuri, U.: The Stage Lives of Animals: Zooesis and Performance. Taylor and Francis (2017)
6. Eguchi, A., Gerardo, H., Twomey, R.: Beyond the black box: human robot interaction through human robot performances. In: Companion of the 2024 ACM/IEEE International Conference on Human-Robot Interaction, HRI '24, pp. 437–441. Association for Computing Machinery (2024). https://doi.org/10.1145/3610978.3640577
7. Gotman, K.: Choreomania: Dance and Disorder. Oxford studies in dance theory. Oxford University Press, Cambridge (2018)
8. Haraway, D.J.: Staying with the trouble: making kin in the Chthulucene. Experimental futures: technological lives, scientific arts, anthropological voices. Duke University Press (2016). https://doi.org/10.1515/9780822373780
9. King, B.: Techno-dramaturgy: meaning-making with machines. In: O'Dwyer, N., Scott, J., Young, G.W. (eds.) Extended Reality Performance: Scenographic Practice in Virtual and Augmented Reality Technologies, 1st edn. Bloomsbury Publishing Plc (2025)

10. Lehmann, H.T., Jürs-Munby, K.: Postdramatic Theatre. Routledge (2006)
11. Ong, J., Twomey, R., Kang, E., Jin, K.J.: Beyond Classification: The Machinic Sublime, pp. 373–379. BCS Learning & Development (2021). https://doi.org/10.14236/ewic/POM2021.50
12. Rouse, M.: From vision to perception: embodied experience in XR performance-making. In: O'Dwyer, N., Scott, J., Young, G.W. (eds.) Extended Reality Performance: Scenographic Practice in Virtual and Augmented Reality Technologies, 1st edn. Bloomsbury Publishing Plc (2025)
13. Schlesinger, T.: Making sense. dramaturgy in times of loss – for my fellow fellows (2025). https://www.akademie-solitude.de/en/making-sense-dramaturgy-in-times-of-loss-for-my-fellow-fellows/
14. Smith, A.E., Bendix, S., Lichtman, D., Twomey, R.: Rehearsing realities: A dramaturgy for co-creating preferable futures (2021)
15. Smith, A.E., Twomey, R.: The future of real-time AI: liveness, co-creation, and participatory play. In: 36th Annual Conference of the Society for Literature, Science and the Arts (SLSA) (2023)
16. Twomey, R.: Communion and cohabitation. In: Kang, E. (ed.) Welcome a New Neighbor, Creative Machine (2022). http://roberttwomey.com/2021/10/book-chapter-communion-and-cohabitation/
17. Twomey, R., Eliza Smith, A., Brockmeier, R., Bendix, S.: Quantum theater: extending realities for post-AI liveness. In: Proceedings of the Special Interest Group on Computer Graphics and Interactive Techniques Conference Spatial Storytelling. SIGGRAPH Spatial Storytelling '25. Association for Computing Machinery (2025). https://doi.org/10.1145/3721244.3742446
18. Zupane Lotker, S.: Interview. Methuen Drama, 1st edn. (2024). https://doi.org/10.5040/9781350349841

Directing Space: Rehearsing Architecture as Performer with Explainable AI

Pavlos Panagiotidis[1]([⊠]) [iD], Jocelyn Spence[1] [iD], Nils Jaeger[2] [iD], and Paul Tennent[1] [iD]

[1] School of Computer Science, University of Nottingham, Nottingham, UK
{pavlos.panagiotidis,jocelyn.spence4,
paul.tennent}@nottingham.ac.uk
[2] Department of Architecture and Built Environment, Faculty of Engineering, University of Nottingham, Nottingham, UK
nils.jaeger@nottingham.ac.uk

Abstract. As AI systems increasingly become embedded in interactive and immersive artistic environments, artists and technologists are discovering new opportunities to engage with their interpretive and autonomous capacities as creative collaborators in live performance. The focus of this work-in-progress is on outlining conceptual and technical foundations under which performance-makers and interactive architecture can collaborate within rehearsal settings. It introduces a rehearsal-oriented prototype system for shaping and testing AI-mediated environments within creative practice. This approach treats interactive architecture as a performative agent that senses spatial behaviour and speech, interprets these signals through a large language model, and generates real-time environmental adaptations. Designed for deployment in physical performance spaces, the system employs virtual blueprints to support iterative experimentation and creative dialogue between artists and AI agents, using reasoning traces to inform architectural interaction design grounded in dramaturgical principles.

Keywords: Interactive Architecture · Dramaturgical AI · Virtual Rehearsal · Explainable AI · Mixed Reality Performance.

1 Introduction

In the novel *The Thousand Dreams of Stellavista* [1], houses absorb the emotional residues of their occupants and respond in kind; the story offers both a critique of technological progress and a provocation to imagine architecture as a reactive character shaped by human behaviour. This idea resonates with contemporary immersive performance, where architecture functions as dramaturgical material: environments frame and guide experience, surrounding audiences who often move freely through space [2, 3], echoing how architecture can be understood less by what it is than by what it does [4]. Building

Author's Accepted Manuscript. Released under the Creative Commons license: Attribution 4.0 International (CC BY 4.0) https://creativecommons.org/licenses/by/4.0/

© The Author(s), under exclusive license to Springer Nature Switzerland AG 2026
K. Woodward et al. (Eds.): CLIP 2026, CCIS 2865, pp. 70–80, 2026.
https://doi.org/10.1007/978-3-032-16893-1_5

Fig. 1. Responsive light adaptation. A prototype demonstrating how the system triggers light adaptation based on human spatial relationships during rehearsal

on this view, we examine how architecture can perform autonomously through AI mediated decision making. Beyond its creative appeal, this approach leverages the capacity of AI structures to handle complex, large-scale input and output flows, coordinating data from multiple rooms, managing numerous actuators in parallel, and analysing long term behavioural patterns. While such systems may lack the subtlety of human interpretation, they afford levels of scalability and continuity unattainable through human operation alone.

We introduce an AI-driven virtual blueprint that guides spatial behaviour through dialogic, dramaturgical interaction, shifting responsive environments from reactive automation toward interpretable, co-creative architectural agency. The blueprint integrates an LLM-based architectural agent into a virtual environment, allowing system behaviour to be shaped through natural language rather than hard-coded rules. This setup allows behavioural tendencies to be established and refined before they are transferred into the physical environment. The current prototype realises the system's foundational elements, using a large language model to interpret dramaturgical input and generate spatial adaptations in a virtual built environment. Additionally, early physical trials link sensors and actuators to their virtual counterparts. As the project progresses, we will examine how artists engage with such systems, how dramaturgical meaning emerges in dialogue with LLM agents, and how reasoning traces can support creative collaboration. Although developed for performance making, the approach also points toward broader applications in socially responsive environments where spaces participate in interaction and co-design processes with their users.

2 Background and Conceptual Foundations

This section outlines the conceptual and methodological foundations of the work. It draws on theatre-making, mixed-reality performance practices and research in virtual scenography. In this context, performance refers to immersive and interactive events where the actions of performers, audiences, and the built environment are witnessed and responded to. The work does not focus on traditional on-stage performance but rather on expanded forms of experiences with theatrical qualities.

Research at the intersection of performance and technology has shown how computation can act as a dramaturgical force, framing interaction as performative and technologies as expressive agents [5–8]. Artistic companies have similarly explored mixed-reality environments where spatial design, adaptive media, and networked technologies are integral to audience experience [9–11].

Building on this trajectory, our framework brings dramaturgical logics into rehearsal within mixed reality systems where theatre-makers collaborate in real time with AI agents that influence the built environment. It extends a previous study that developed a no-code, rule-based authoring tool for responsive environments in a devising process [12]. Devising is a collaborative, improvisation-based method of theatre-making where performances emerge through exploration rather than a predetermined script. The tool was designed to make experimentation with responsive spaces faster and more intuitive, reducing reliance on technologists and keeping creative iteration within rehearsal. Performers linked gestures, positions, and vocal expressions sensed through computer vision and audio analysis to architectural adaptations, triggering scenographic responses such as light changes based on predefined mappings (Fig. 1). This enabled theatre devisers to explore how embodied relations could shape spatial behaviour, though responsiveness remained limited to explicitly defined rules. The current system aims to address this limitation by allowing theatre-makers to express intentions in natural language, with the LLM improvising responses in the form of environmental adaptations.

Yet enabling such collaboration in practice introduces several methodological and practical challenges, as performance-making is often limited by the scale and cost of building scenographic environments solely to test interaction logic. Virtual environments offer a way to explore possibilities without premature physical construction. Prior work in 3D, VR, and digital twin technologies shows how virtual models can function as prototypes [13, 14] and how collaborative environments can function as shared rehearsal spaces [15–17]. In our approach, simulation enables experimentation with interactions guided by the AI agent itself. While Wizard-of-Oz methods [18] can only approximate system behaviour, a virtual model with an embedded AI agent allows the interaction logic to be shaped and rehearsed before deployment. Once the creative team settles the desired behaviour in the virtual prototype, this logic can be transferred to the physical setup by linking real sensors and actuators to their virtual counterparts, allowing the interaction to continue in the physical environment.

For AI agents to take part meaningfully in rehearsal, they need to perceive events, simulated or real, as having dramaturgical significance. They should be able to recognise them in a way that at least comes close to how human collaborators experience them in live rehearsal. The problem is that many performance practices involve subtle, layered behaviours that are not easy for machines to read. For example, frameworks such as

Laban Movement Analysis can be used to describe movement qualities [19], but the very nature of these qualities makes them hard to translate into computational terms [20]. For this reason, we turn to two performance-making methods that include actions and events which, although cannot be fully reduced to data, they can make observation easier for the kinds of AI systems we have today. We refer to examples such as spatial relationships, topographies, and gestures from *Viewpoints* [21], as well as zones of attention, voids, and gravitational points from immersive theatre-making [3].

Furthermore, we draw on the foundational rehearsal logic developed by Stanislavski, which includes backstories, objectives, and given circumstances to support the dramaturgical framing of interactions [22, 23]. Although it is perhaps one of the most subtle and complex dramaturgical frameworks, we see potential in how it can be expressed through directing instructions, discussions, and rehearsal notes. This means that it may help form a basis for describing dramaturgical frames to the LLM-based system through language, although how far this can go remains to be seen in practice.

Our system operationalises these theatrical logics through three components:

1. a sensing layer that perceives behaviour, using overhead computer vision for position tracking with YOLOv8 [24] and speech analysis on recorded audio using Vosk [25]
2. a large language model accessed through OpenAI's 4o Model API [26] that interprets dramaturgical intent from open ended directions
3. a Unity [27] based virtual environment that functions as a rehearsal space for testing and refining interactions before physical deployment, currently connected to Philips Hue smart lighting for environmental actuation [28].

When the system makes choices—currently limited to changing lighting configurations with potential extensions to sound cues or moving objects—an explainability layer exposes its reasoning through a textual trace. This trace allows directors and designers to review decisions and adjust dramaturgical inputs in an iterative, "ping-pong" rehearsal between human and system. It addresses a common problem in interactive AI, where opaque system behaviour hinders collaboration [29], by keeping reasoning visible. It remains to be seen to what extent the reasoning trace supports the creative process, since it functions as a post hoc rationalisation of the system's decisions rather than a direct account of its reasoning. A later stage of this study will focus on how such explanations, even if partial or approximate, can assist creative practitioners in shaping and directing the system's behaviour. Taken together, these components form the groundwork for an LLM-mediated interactive architectural system for immersive performance-making. The following section outlines the system's structure and operation.

3 Interaction Generation Flow

3.1 Staging a Collaborative System

The system is presented here as an evolving prototype developed in *Unity* [27]. We outline both its current capabilities and its intended future development. It is capable of perceiving real or simulated data and triggering responses in the virtual blueprint, and eventually in the physical space. Its capacity to operate in a rehearsal simulation mode, where virtual agents and synthetic speech emulate performer and audience behaviour

(Fig. 2, top left), is designed to allow creatives to explore and refine how the AI responds to dramaturgical framing. It enables them to test different scenarios and observe its reactions without the constant need for live participants or physical setups. Position data are also aggregated into a dynamic heat grid that visualises patterns of movement and attention, allowing both system and users to detect zones of concentrated activity or "hotspots" (Fig. 2, top right).

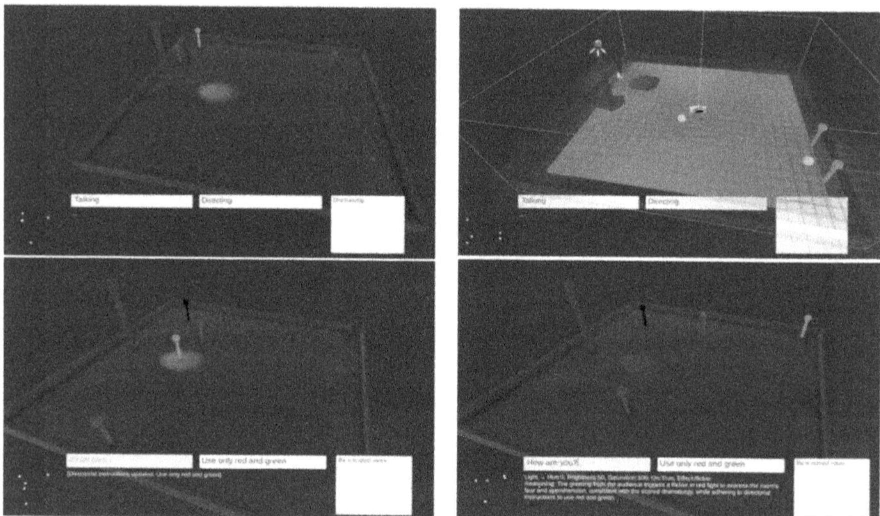

Fig. 2. System responses and visualization modes. Top left: virtual lighting cue where a green light activates when a virtual spectator approaches the pillar. Top right: audience heatmap with red indicating high activity, blue low, and yellow marking gravitational points. Bottom left: dramaturgical or directorial prompts where the system is instructed to "be a scared room" and "use only red and green." Bottom right: LLM reasoning trace showing the system's response to "How are you?" through a red light and the explanation "The greeting triggers red light to express fear, consistent with the scared dramaturgy and red–green instruction."

Beyond the sensing and the actuation layers, the system includes a dramaturgical layer through which the designer or director defines a creative frame to guide its behaviour. While explicit behavioural rules can still be specified, this approach feels largely exhausted, conceptually if not technically. Instead of just prescribing actions, this layer can be used to offer a short narrative or contextual prompt that gives the environment a sense of prior experience, motivation, or emotional tone—effectively directing the system's "inner world" and assigning the AI a dramaturgical standpoint from which to generate interaction (Fig. 2, bottom left). When the system makes a decision, for example changing a light because a participant said something, it explains its reasoning (Fig. 2, bottom right) to help the practitioner refine its behaviour through further prompting.

These layers (real and simulated inputs, decision engine, and actuators) are already functional within the current prototype. In its full configuration, the AI will integrate the dialogic interaction described in the following sections to deepen the dramaturgy guiding the system's behaviour in live rehearsal.

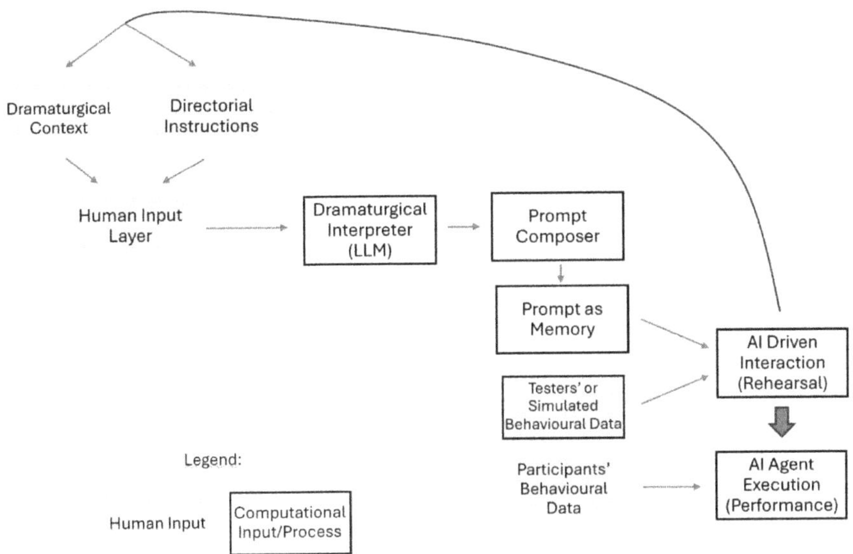

Fig. 3. Interaction generation pipeline. The system synthesises dramaturgical and directorial inputs, interpretive analysis, and accumulated rehearsal memory into a single consolidated prompt defining the AI agent's performative behaviour.

3.2 Dramaturgical Interpreter

Building on the dramaturgical layer, the system is being extended with an interpreter that translates open-ended dramaturgical descriptions into more concrete parameters. For example, a director might prompt: "You are the house from *The Thousand Dreams of Stellavista* [1]. You have witnessed turbulent relationships, absorbed traces of jealousy and loss, and now respond cautiously to emotional tension in the room." Such framing does not prescribe actions but situates the system within a narrative perspective.

The interpreter analyses the text to extract dramaturgically relevant features—objectives ("protect itself from emotional harm"), affective tones ("cautious, melancholic"), or environmental metaphors ("the space tightens when tension rises"). It may also engage the director in brief clarification, for instance asking whether the room's caution should be expressed as a withdrawal of light or as tightening illumination. It will also be interesting to see how different LLM models handle this kind of dialogue, and how much guidance or fine-tuning they might need to engage meaningfully with dramaturgical direction. Each model may approach the dialogue differently, deciding what to focus on and what to leave out, and it will be important to observe how well they can use what they find to inform the actuation. Internally, this information is stored in a lightweight data schema that defines relationships between intention, affect, and spatial behaviour, as shown below (for illustrative purposes):

- "intention": "respond cautiously to emotional tension"
- "affect": " subdued calm",
- "metaphor": "tightening space",
- "primary_modality": "light",
- "reaction_pattern": "gradual dimming under high energy"

3.3 Directorial Layer

Sitting above the dramaturgical interpreter, the directorial layer provides more precise control over the system's behaviour. Unlike the dramaturgical layer, which invites interpretation, this mode aims to treat each instruction as a concrete command to be executed. The director may, for example, specify: "When someone enters a room, fade all side lights to 30 percent intensity," or "Trigger the fan when two participants stand within two metres of each other." In this mode, the system does not infer broader meaning but focuses solely on the accurate execution of the given cues.

A potentially useful application of this layer may emerge during live performance. When a director, orchestrator, or even a performer experiences an unexpected situation that requires the environment to adjust in a specific way, this layer can be used in real time to issue clear, language-based instructions to the system. For instance, if the system turns off the lights in a certain area, the director may command, "Turn the lights back on in Room B," prompting an immediate response. It is important to note that, in such cases, the purpose is not to override the system (or replace any dedicated safety overrides that may be in place) but to maintain the behaviour within the logic of the spatial performer system.

3.4 Dramaturgical Memory

In rehearsal, the two layers operate together. During, or after each run, the director or designer reviews the system's reasoning traces and provides new instructions, much like in a traditional rehearsal, indicating what worked and what needs adjustment. These notes are incorporated into the next iteration of the loop, guiding the AI to refine its dramaturgical policies. Through successive cycles, the human and system co-evolve a shared vocabulary of interaction, and the environment gradually develops a dramaturgical memory (Fig. 3).

This memory comprises accumulated instructions, distilled notes, and behavioural traces from rehearsal runs, capturing both the dialogue between director and system and the patterns emerging through interaction. Rather than storing information indiscriminately, the system filters and organises data according to dramaturgical relevance and the director's guidance. The exact mechanism through which this dramaturgical memory will operate will depend on the type and volume of data the system needs to handle. A simple implementation could rely on iterative filtering, using an LLM to analyse rehearsal information according to predefined prompts and generate a consolidated dramaturgical summary. In cases where the data become too large or complex to be processed directly, a retrieval-augmented generation (RAG) approach might be necessary.

The memory operates on two levels. The short-term layer prioritises recent exchanges, enabling the system to respond coherently to ongoing dialogue, while the long-term layer preserves distilled elements central to the evolving dramaturgy. By retaining and weighting this information, the system can remember its own creative history and recognise recurring patterns. This allows it to anticipate familiar situations and adjust its interpretive stance in later rehearsals. This dramaturgical memory forms the connective tissue between individual sessions, allowing the AI to grow contextually aware rather than restart with each new interaction. At the end of each rehearsal phase, the system consolidates its learning into a single dramaturgical prompt that summarises the refined behavioural tendencies, cues, and interpretive logic developed during rehearsal. This prompt (Fig. 4) acts as the environment's "score" and can later be executed in a physical setting using real sensors and actuators. When transferred to the real space, the system continues to log its decisions and the corresponding audience responses, capturing data on how people move, speak, and react to the environment's behaviour. These logs create a feedback archive that allows the team to replay and analyse specific moments of interaction for further refinement.

```
[DRAMATURGICAL CONTEXT]                        [ACTION]
You are the house from Ballard's *The
Thousand Dreams of Stellavista*.               Dim the light to a soft red.

You have absorbed traces of jealousy and       [REASONING]
loss, and you now respond cautiously
to emotional tension in the room.              The greeting introduces mild
                                               emotional openness.

[DIRECTORIAL RULES]                            Since the room is cautious, it
- Use only red and green light.                should acknowledge the voice without
                                               overwhelming it.
- Make all transitions last at least 3
seconds.

- When someone speaks near the pillar,
reduce light intensity slightly.


[CURRENT ENVIRONMENTAL STATE]
- Two participants near the pillar.

- Recent speech detected: "How are you?"

- Overall activity increasing in the front
area.
```

Fig. 4. Illustrative prompt showing how dramaturgical, directorial, and environmental inputs merge into a single instruction (left), guiding the AI's interpretive response (right). Simplified for explanatory purposes.

The system has not yet undergone formal evaluation, but early informal testing indicates that it responds relatively consistently and with low latency across both virtual and physical setups. The simulated version presented in Fig. 2 and an equivalent physical setup were used to explore basic interaction patterns, with the LLM producing colour and light intensity adaptations in response to textual or spoken input. In these tests the system was able to interpret simple framings, maintain short-term behavioural tendencies, and sustain basic colour based communication patterns, such as consistently using specific colours for affirmation or refusal during a dialogue. These early observations suggest that the core interaction loop functions reliably, although more complex dramaturgical behaviour will require systematic study. It can also articulate its reasons in ways that make sense within very simple dramaturgical frames (see Fig. 2), but the structures required for sustained creative dialogue have not yet been developed.

4 Discussion

This work proposes a space-as-performer perspective, building on research into adaptive architectural systems that evolve with their occupants [30]. Beyond creative curiosity—the impulse to "play with an AI room"—the prototype investigates how AI systems can achieve scalable perception and actuation beyond human operational limits. While human operators can perceive nuance and respond sensitively to complex cues, they remain constrained by the amount and simultaneity of information they can process. At scale, however, an AI-driven environment can coordinate actions across multiple rooms, audiences, and timeframes, detecting spatial and behavioural patterns that would remain unnoticed by human operators. This reflects views of distributed cognition, where collective systems sustain levels of parallelism and coordination beyond individual capacity [31], and extends into a notion of pervasive computing as an ambient infrastructure through which computation operates creatively and autonomously within architectural complexity—here framed within an immersive dramaturgy.

Despite this potential, shared vocabularies and workflows for engaging AI-driven environments as creative partners in immersive theatre remain limited. Our proposed LLM-driven interactive architectural system addresses this gap by functioning as a collaborator—directable and interpretable rather than merely reactive. Treating the built environment as a co-performer within collaborative performance-making shifts design from human control toward shared initiative, consistent with enacted views of ensemble as corporeal and material coordination across bodies, matter, intention, and atmosphere [32]. For example, one could imagine sprawling immersive works such as those of *Punchdrunk* being assisted in both devising and performances distributed across dozens of rooms by such a system once it is fully explored and tested.

In line with approaches that enable parallel autonomy between human users and digital agents—shown to sustain collaboration without overdetermining it or increasing cognitive load [13]—this work introduces a dialogic space for iterative virtual rehearsal with the AI agent. Here, explainability takes the form of decision justifications, acting as part of the dramaturgical dialogue where reasoning traces function as rehearsal notes rather than technical diagnostics. Building on approaches such as Human-Centered Explainable AI [29], we will examine which forms of explanation best support direction and guidance, and when they become distracting. Early prototype versions of the system suggest that simulation can serve as a low-risk stage for exploring interaction dynamics before technical or spatial commitments are fixed. Using the same sensing and reasoning pipeline across virtual and physical contexts positions the blueprint as a testbed for interaction rather than a visualisation, pointing toward mixed-reality staging where physical and digital elements coexist [7].

Although the sensing and actuation modules have been developed, current trials remain confined to simulation. The dramaturgical interpreter (LLM) also requires further refinement to ensure stability in live rehearsal contexts. A key question is how interactions rehearsed in virtual blueprints translate to physical environments. The absence of material presence and embodied resistance in simulation may limit how intuition and spatial understanding carry over to real space. Additionally, LLMs may have limited spatial and temporal reasoning, leading to inconsistencies in timing or dramaturgical coherence; in such cases, rule-based control may be safer. Ethical considerations are also central, as the system logs behavioural data, requiring transparent consent, anonymisation, and responsible data handling.

5 Conclusion

This paper has outlined the conceptual and technical foundations of a rehearsal-oriented framework for directing and rehearsing AI-mediated environments. The next stage of the work will focus on how artists engage with the system as a creative partner. Through performance-led research we will examine how they direct, adapt, and repurpose the AI's dramaturgical behaviour across rehearsal and performance contexts, observing how creative language, reasoning traces, and system feedback shape their process. These studies will serve both to refine the interpretive stability of the LLM and to identify the kinds of collaborative vocabularies that support co-direction between humans and spatial AI systems. Our interest extends to potential applications beyond artistic contexts, exploring how such frameworks may align with dialogic and anticipatory creative AI [33] and inform the design of responsive cultural, educational, or even therapeutic environments where autonomous spatial systems actively participate in interaction.

Acknowledgments. This work was supported by the Engineering and Physical Sciences Research Council [EP/T022493/1], by Lakeside Arts, by Makers of Imaginary Worlds, and by the Horizon Centre for Doctoral Training at the University of Nottingham.

Disclosure of Interests. The authors have no competing interests to declare that are relevant to the content of this article.

References

1. Ballard, J.G.: The Voices of Time and Other Stories. Berkley Medallion, New York (1962)
2. Machon, J.: Immersive Theatres: Intimacy and Immediacy in Contemporary Performance. Palgrave Macmillan, New York (2013)
3. Warren J.: Creating Worlds: How to Make Immersive Theatre. Nick Hern Books (2017)
4. Leatherbarrow, D.: Architecture's unscripted performance. In: Kolarevic, B., Malkawi, A. (eds.) Performative Architecture: Beyond Instrumentality, pp. 6–19. Spon Press, New York (2005)
5. Laurel B.: Computers as Theatre, 2nd edn. Addison-Wesley Professional (2013)
6. Dixon S.: Digital Performance. MIT Press (2007)
7. Benford, S., Giannachi, G.: Performing Mixed Reality. MIT Press, Cambridge (2011)
8. Spence, J.: Performative Experience Design. Springer (2016)
9. Rimini Protokoll: Situation Rooms, Berlin (2013)
10. Blast Theory. https://www.blasttheory.co.uk/. Accessed 19 Oct 2025
11. Punchdrunk: Viola's Room, London (2024)

12. Panagiotidis, P., Spence, J., Jaeger, N.: Devising experiments with interactive environments. Presented at Performing Space 2025, Nafplio, Greece, 4–7 July 2025. arXiv:2511.11229 (2025). https://doi.org/10.48550/arXiv.2511.11229. Proceedings forthcoming
13. Del Favero, D., Thurow, S., Wallen, L.: The iDesign platform: immersive intelligent aesthetics for scenographic modelling. Theatre Perform. Des. **7**, 82–95 (2021). https://doi.org/10.1080/23322551.2021.1919488
14. Kirjavainen, E., Kalving, M., Etto, J., Colley, A.: Exploring the use of a digital twin in theatre stage design. In: Proceedings of the IASDR 2023 Conference. University of Lapland, Rovaniemi, Finland (2023). https://doi.org/10.21606/iasdr.2023.806
15. Cegys, P., Weijdom, J.: Mixing realities: reflections on presence and embodiment in intermedial performance design of Blue Hour VR. Theatre Perform. Des. **6**, 81–101 (2020). https://doi.org/10.1080/23322551.2020.1785710
16. McKendrick, Z., Somin, L., Finn, P., Sharlin, E.: Virtual rehearsal suite. In: Proceedings of the 2023 ACM International Conference on Interactive Media Experiences, pp. 27–39. ACM, New York (2023)
17. Xylakis, E., Tsamis, K., Vatsolakis, C., et al.: VR Prova. In: Proceedings of the 3rd International Conference of the ACM Greek SIGCHI Chapter, pp. 153–158. ACM, New York (2025)
18. Dahlbäck, N., Jönsson, A., Ahrenberg, L.: Wizard of Oz studies why and how. Knowl. Based Syst. **6**, 258–266 (1993). https://doi.org/10.1016/0950-7051(93)90017-N
19. Durupinar, F.: Perception of human motion similarity based on Laban movement analysis. In: ACM Symposium on Applied Perception 2021. ACM, New York (2021)
20. Lockyer, M., Bartram, L.R., Schiphorst, T., Studd, K.: Extending computational models of abstract motion with movement qualities. In: Proceedings of the 2nd International Workshop on Movement and Computing (MOCO 2015), pp. 92–99. Association for Computing Machinery, Vancouver, Canada (2015). https://doi.org/10.1145/2790994.2791008
21. Bogart, A., Landau, T.: The Viewpoints Book. Theatre Communications Group, New York (2005)
22. Merlin, B.: The Complete Stanislavsky Toolkit. Nick Hern Books, London (2014)
23. Stanislavski, K.: An Actor Prepares. Theatre Arts, New York (1936)
24. Ultralytics: YOLOv8 Toolkit. https://github.com/ultralytics/ultralytics. Accessed 14 Nov 2025
25. Alpha Cephei: Vosk Speech Recognition Toolkit. https://github.com/alphacep/vosk Accessed 14 Nov 2025
26. OpenAI: OpenAI API Documentation Model 4o. https://platform.openai.com/docs. Accessed 14 Nov 2025
27. Unity Technologies: Unity Game Engine. https://unity.com. Accessed 14 Nov 2025
28. Signify: Philips Hue Developer Documentation. https://developers.meethue.com. Accessed 14 Nov 2025
29. Ehsan, U., Riedl, M.O.: Human centered explainable AI. In: HCI International 2020 – Late Breaking Papers, pp. 449–466. Springer, Cham (2020)
30. Gorbet, R.B., Memarian, M., Chan, M., Kulic, D., Beesley, P.: Evolving systems within immersive architectural environments. In: NGB#2: Info-Matter, ed. Nimish Biloria, co-ed. Matias del Campo. Living Architecture Systems Group, in press (2016)
31. Hutchins, E.: Cognition in the Wild. MIT Press (1995)
32. Johnson, G.L., Peterson, B.J., Ingalls, T., Wei, S.X.: Lanterns. In: Proceedings of the 5th International Conference on Movement and Computing, pp. 1–4 (2018)
33. Choi, S.K., DiPaola, S., Gabora, L.: Art and the artificial. J. Creativity **33**, 100069 (2023). https://doi.org/10.1016/j.yjoc.2023.100069

Creative AI Tools and Interfaces

TalkSketch: Multimodal Generative AI for Real-Time Sketch Ideation with Speech

Weiyan Shi[1], Sunaya Upadhyay[2], Geraldine Quek[1], and Kenny Tsu Wei Choo[1(✉)]

[1] Singapore University of Technology and Design, Singapore, Singapore
geraldine_quek@sutd.edu.sg, kennytwchoo@gmail.com, weiyanshi6@gmail.com
[2] Carnegie Mellon University, Pittsburgh, PA, USA
sunayau@andrew.cmu.edu

Abstract. Sketching is a widely used medium for generating and exploring early-stage design concepts. While generative AI (GenAI) chatbots are increasingly used for idea generation, designers often struggle to craft effective prompts and find it difficult to express evolving visual concepts through text alone. In the formative study (N=6), we examined how designers use GenAI during ideation, revealing that text-based prompting disrupts creative flow. To address these issues, we developed TALKSKETCH, an embedded multimodal AI sketching system that integrates freehand drawing with real-time speech input. TALKSKETCH aims to support a more fluid ideation process through capturing verbal descriptions during sketching and generating context-aware AI responses. Our work highlights the potential of GenAI tools to engage the design process itself rather than focusing on output.

Keywords: generative AI · sketching · talking · creativity support

1 Introduction

During early-stage design, sketching plays a central role as an improvisational, open-ended, and dynamic practice [24, 34]. Designers frequently switch between design phases and iterate their sketches to explore alternatives and refine ideas toward promising directions [6]. To enhance efficiency in this formative stage, researchers have explored integrating generative AI (GenAI) [15] into sketch-based design workflows [10, 25, 44, 47]. With advances in multimodal large language models (LLMs), GenAI now offers stronger creative capabilities [39, 42, 48], making it increasingly suitable for supporting designers in early-stage ideation.

However, despite the growing use of GenAI chatbots in idea generation, designers often struggle to craft effective prompts and to express evolving visual concepts through text alone. This command-based interaction paradigm [33] places the burden on designers to direct the system, overlooking other forms of input that may be more natural and intuitive during creative work [21, 30]. In practice, designers often verbalise ideas spontaneously while sketching, yet such contextual cues are rarely captured by current systems.

© The Author(s), under exclusive license to Springer Nature Switzerland AG 2026
K. Woodward et al. (Eds.): CLIP 2026, CCIS 2865, pp. 83–97, 2026.
https://doi.org/10.1007/978-3-032-16893-1_6

To better understand these challenges, we conducted a formative study (N=6) examining how designers use existing GenAI tools for early-stage sketch ideation. Our findings revealed that text-based prompting often interrupts creative flow and creates a disconnect between ideation and sketching activities.

Based on these insights, we developed TalkSketch, a sketching interface with a multimodal AI chatbot that enables users to draw and verbalise ideas simultaneously. TalkSketch captures designers' spoken descriptions during sketching and generates contextually relevant AI responses, aiming to support a more fluid and natural ideation process.

Our research contributes:

1. Findings from a formative study (N=6) revealing key challenges designers face when using current GenAI tools for early-stage sketch ideation.
2. TALKSKETCH: a sketching interface with a multimodal AI chatbot that enables users to draw and verbalize ideas simultaneously.

2   Related Work

2.1   Multimodal Human – AI Interaction for Creative Ideation

Conversational User Interfaces (CUIs) enable dialogue-based interaction that mimics human conversation [27] and are widely deployed in chatbots [13] and voice-activated assistants such as Amazon Alexa and Apple's Siri [4]. Recent advances in Generative AI (GenAI) [11,35], including large language models (LLMs) such as ChatGPT [28] and multimodal assistants such as Gemini [37], have made conversational human – AI interaction broadly accessible and flexible. These tools are increasingly applied in domains such as education [32], healthcare [18], and creative work [3,45], supporting users through natural language dialogue.

A central concern in these systems is whether users can express intent clearly and efficiently. Prior work has explored multimodal input and interface strategies to improve intent communication. Hu et al. [19] introduced *GesPrompt*, which combines co-speech gestures with voice input to enable more natural intent expression in extended reality environments. Cho et al. [9] proposed *Persistent Assistant*, integrating embodied input and multimodal feedback for seamless everyday interactions. Other work embeds LLMs into direct manipulation environments, mapping graphical user interface actions or visual edits into structured prompts [3,26], showing that embedding language models within interactive contexts can reduce the burden of verbose prompting. Yet, most of these systems are designed for short, directive, or domain-specific tasks such as code editing or data visualisation, rather than open-ended creative ideation.

In design, creativity-support tools increasingly integrate GenAI into mainstream workflows. Commercial platforms such as Adobe Firefly [2], Canva Magic Studio [7], and Figma AI [12] demonstrate how generative models assist in rapid visual exploration, while research prototypes extend this trend toward more expressive input. For example, *DesignPrompt* [29] allows designers to compose prompts using text, colour, and imagery, and *DesignWeaver* [36] introduces palette-based refinement to support iterative design. Similarly, sketch-based interfaces such as *Inkspire* [25] and *SketchAI* [10] demonstrate how free-hand input can guide image generation and support analogical inspiration.

Despite these developments, two key gaps remain. First, existing multimodal CUIs focus primarily on explicit prompts and discrete commands, overlooking more spontaneous forms of intent expression such as speech or thinking aloud during creative work. Second, current creativity-support tools rely mainly on visual and textual input, rarely considering how spoken language—produced naturally during sketching—might complement visual ideation.

Our work addresses these gaps by investigating how combining speech and sketch input can support fluid, multimodal interaction with GenAI during early-stage design ideation.

2.2   Talking as a Novel Input Modality for Sketching

Speech is also a natural modality for externalising thought, long recognised in systems such as *SHRDLU* [41] and *Put-That-There* [5] from the 1970-80 s. It enables real-time, low-friction expression of ideas, making it especially valuable in early-stage design when thoughts are fluid and evolving [14]. Sketching and speech together can serve as two intuitive, complementary interaction methods in design and creative domains, allowing users to express nuances that one modality alone might omit [1].

Recent works demonstrate how combining sketch and speech supports more natural and expressive communication: Rosenberg et al. [31] introduced *DrawTalking*, which combines sketching with storytelling through speech to construct interactive animated worlds, while Giunchi et al. [16] showed that integrating sketch and speech for 3D model retrieval in virtual environments helped overcome the limitations of sketch-only input. Cheng et al. [8] also explored speech and sketch as inputs for enhancing communication with AI through context awareness in an exploratory Wizard-of-Oz study.

While prior research highlights how speech can enhance collaboration with AI, the impact of naturally produced speech during sketching on subsequent GenAI interactions remains unexplored. Our work therefore systematically investigates sketching-while-talking as a combined input modality for early-stage design ideation. Rather than treating sketching and speech as separate channels, we integrate both within a multimodal LLM chatbot to examine whether verbal descriptions and visual strokes together can improve AI alignment with user intent.

3   Formative Study: Understanding Early-Stage Design Workflow with GenAI

We first conducted a formative study, combining a design task with interviews, to understand how designers integrate GenAI into early-stage design and to identify opportunities for multimodal AI support to inform our subsequent system design in Sect. 4. Our institution's ethics review board approved this study, and we obtained informed consent from all participants.

Participants. We recruited six participants (2 female, 4 male) with a basic background in design; at the very least, they had completed one design-related course (e.g., *Urban Sketching* or *Design Thinking and Innovation*). The participants included three students, two entry-level designers, and one experienced design practitioner, with design backgrounds spanning architecture, furniture, interior, robotics, and electronic product design. All participants had 2–5 years of part/full-time experience in design. They received approximately USD 7.8 as compensation for completing the 1-hour study.

Study Protocol. The study consists of three parts: pre-task interview (10 min), design task (30 min), and post-task interview (20 min). The pre-task interview captures participants' design backgrounds, sketching habits, and prior experiences with GenAI tools. For the design task, we asked participants to design a household bread toaster and to express as many design ideas as possible under 30 min using a sketching application such as Goodnotes[1] or Procreate[2]. They were permitted to utilize their personal devices–to ensure a familiar arrangement–or our Apple iPad Pro 13" and Apple Pencil set up with popular sketching apps (e.g., Goodnotes, Procreate) and GenAI tools (e.g., ChatGPT (GPT-4o)[3], Gemini[4], Midjourney[5]). The post-task interview then examined participants' views on the AI's role in supporting or limiting ideation, and captured their aspirations and expectations for an "ideal" AI assistant.

Data Analysis. We analysed the qualitative data by examining both participants' interactions with sketching and AI tools during the design tasks and their reflections in post-study interviews. This allowed us to capture overall usage patterns, such as how participants sketched, engaged with GenAI tools, and iterated on ideas, while also identifying the challenges and gaps they experienced with current tools. These insights inform the design goals of our system.

3.1   Overall Usage Patterns and Challenges

We observed three recurring usage patterns in how participants incorporated GenAI into early-stage ideation during the design task. These patterns, along with the reported challenges, surfaced during the post-interview.

---

[1] https://www.goodnotes.com/
[2] https://procreate.com/
[3] https://chatgpt.com/
[4] https://gemini.google.com/app
[5] https://midjourney.com

Pattern 1: Using GenAI for Research and Ideation. Participants often used ChatGPT to explore design problems, define target users, or to inspire new directions. For instance, P1 asked about commonly found toaster issues and focused on cleaning functions, while P3 explored different user groups to inspire persona-driven designs. These uses supported functional exploration, but initial AI responses were often *"too generic"* (P3) and only became actionable after repeated prompt refinement.

Pattern 2: Using GenAI to Render Sketch-Based Ideas. Several participants uploaded their sketches to ChatGPT Image or Gemini, or relied on text prompts, to visualise concepts. For instance, P2 uploaded a sideways-eject sketch, while P5 asked Gemini for a toaster with butter and egg compartments. However, the outputs often failed to match intent. P1 described the results as *"kind of crazy,"* P2 concluded, *"I might have to redraw the whole thing so AI can understand,"* and P5 added, *"It takes too much time, I'd rather just draw."* Many participants ultimately returned to manual sketching for better clarity and control.

Pattern 3: Iterative Loops Across Sketching, Prompting, and Referencing. Participants often moved back and forth between tools. P3 only used text in ChatGPT to imagine playful forms (e.g., cat- or book-shaped toasters), while P1 first researched in ChatGPT, then sketched, went back to sketching after clarifications, and finally tried rendering images. P1 noted that *"uploading sketches to ChatGPT was not so easy to operate on iPad."* This reflected how tool-switching slowed the process and introduced friction, especially for those who wanted to use image generation (P1, P2, P5, P6).

Challenges Across Patterns. Across these usage patterns, participants encountered three main challenges: (1) AI responses that were too generic or required extensive refinement, (2) mismatched or low-quality image outputs that failed to convey intent, and (3) fragmented workflows due to frequent switching between different tools. These issues often interrupted the ideation flow and made participants rely more heavily on manual sketching for clarity and control.

3.2   Design Goals for TALKSKETCH

During the post-interview, participants proposed several workflow improvements to enhance the usefulness and usability of AI tools in early-stage design, particularly in terms of integration, input flexibility, and contextual responsiveness.

Goal 1: Integrate AI with Sketching Tools. Rather than operating AI separately, participants hoped for tighter integration of AI within their sketching environment. P5 imagined an AI assistant *"embedded directly into sketching app"* that could notice overlooked design opportunities or recommend new features. P6 likewise wanted the AI to interpret her rough visuals directly and *"add internal or functional details"* on top of her own sketches. They expressed that embedded support would reduce switching between tools and allow AI to respond more fluidly to real-time ideation.

Goal 2: Reduce Designers' Fatigue with Long Prompts. Many participants (P2, P5, P6) expressed fatigue from repeatedly typing long prompts to clarify their intent. P2 admitted he was *"too lazy to retype the whole thing,"* while P5 preferred to *"just draw"* instead of describing every detail. Participants advocated for expanded input modalities such as annotated sketches, voice commands, or real-time drawing, as alternatives to laborious text input. P6, for instance, envisioned being able to sketch a toaster form and have the AI *"fill in the mechanism"* without extra explanation. Such input flexibility would better match their natural workflows and reduce prompt clarification during ideation.

Goal 3: A More Proactive and Context-Aware AI. Participants wanted AI to behave less like a passive tool and more like a design partner capable of understanding the user's intent. P3 proposed that the assistant *"should know what I'm trying to do"* P4 suggested that AI should *"see what I'm drawing and just give suggestions,"* and suggested a friendly avatar that feels more responsive and approachable. P2 imagined a system that could *"first discuss the sketch with me"* before trying to render anything, to avoid miscommunication. This desire for AI's proactivity includes the ability to respond to ambiguous sketches, partial ideas, or evolving concepts in real time, without relying solely on explicit step-by-step instructions.

4   TALKSKETCH: System Design and Development

We first describe the technical implementation of TALKSKETCH (Fig. 1), which integrates three core components: a digital sketching canvas for creating and managing drawings, to address the goal of integrating GenAI into sketching tools (Sect. 3.2 Goal 1); a speech capture module that transcribes the user's speech during sketching, aiming to support the goal of reducing fatigue from long prompts (Sect. 3.2 Goal 2); and a multimodal AI chatbot that combines automatic insights with interactive text and image generation, aiming to make AI more proactive and context-aware (Sect. 3.2 Goal 3). We then illustrate how these components work together through a system walkthrough using a concept toaster design example (Fig. 2).

4.1   Technical Implementations

TALKSKETCH integrates a unified multimodal AI chatbot that aims to support both proactive and user-initiated interaction. It comprises three complementary modules: Sketching, Talking, and Multimodal AI Chatbot.

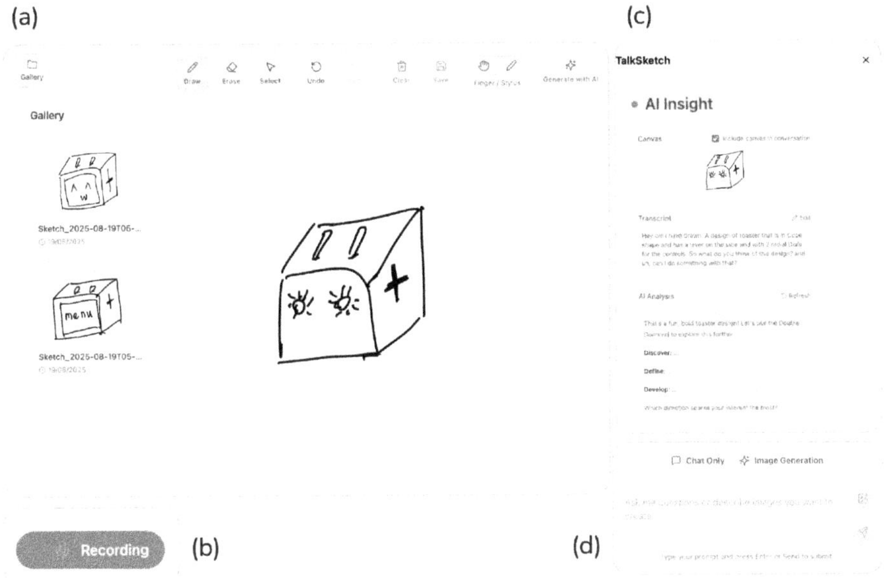

Fig. 1. Overview of the TALKSKETCH system interface. *(a)* **Sketching** module: Users draw product concepts (e.g., a toaster) using stylus input on the canvas. The interface includes a sketch gallery, drawing toolbar, and a button to launch the **Multimodal AI Chatbot**. *(b)* **Talking** module: Voice recording captures the user's thinking aloud during sketching. *(c)* AI Insight panel shows automatic feedback based on the sketch and spoken transcript. *(d)* Text and image generation interface for multimodal interaction with the AI. Together, (c) and (d) constitute the **Multimodal AI Chatbot** module.

Sketching Module. The sketching canvas (Fig. 1a) serves as the central workspace where participants draw early-stage design ideas using a stylus or touch input. Built using *Fabric.js*[6], the canvas supports drawing, erasing, selection, undo/redo, and canvas reset as illustrated in Fig. 1. The top toolbar consolidates essential drawing controls along with the *Generate with AI* button. To facilitate interaction between users and AI, users can select any region of the sketching canvas and export it into the chatbot as part of a multimodal prompt. The *Save to Gallery* button allows users to save their canvas to the gallery once they are content with it; saved canvases can also be retrieved through the *Gallery*.

Talking Module. TALKSKETCH augments the sketching experience with real-time voice capture to support think-aloud workflows. Audio recording initiates automatically when users are sketching (without the chatbot open), and the recording symbol will be turned on simultaneously to indicate this. Once the user

---

[6] http://fabricjs.com/

opens the AI Chatbot, the recording stops and the captured audio is streamed for low-latency transcription via Google Cloud Speech-to-Text[7].

Multimodal AI Chatbot Module. The multimodal AI chatbot (see Figs. 1c and 1d) has two main components: (1) *AI Insights*, which automatically generate reflective feedback based on user sketches and verbal ideation, and (2) a *Multimodal Chatbot Interface*, where users can engage the AI through both text and sketch input. Both components share a common back-end powered by the *Gemini* series of multimodal models[8], known for their strong cross-modal reasoning capabilities and broad adoption across creative and analytical tasks [37,43]. Specifically, the text-based conversational features are supported by Gemini 2.0 Flash, while image generation is handled by Gemini 2.5 Flash Image. Both models accept multimodal inputs such as text and images, but they serve different purposes. Gemini 2.0 Flash is a fast multimodal-reasoning variant that produces text-only output, whereas Gemini 2.5 Flash Image is an image-generation variant of the Gemini 2.5 family, specialised for producing high-quality images from multimodal prompts. The *Multimodal AI Chatbot Module* maintains a unified conversation history that persists throughout the entire session and is consistently shared across both models, ensuring coherent context when switching between text and image generation.

The first feature of the Multimodal AI Chatbot, **AI Insights** (Fig. 1c), provides proactive, structured, and reflective feedback based on the user's current sketch and verbal input. It is automatically triggered when the user clicks on *Generate with AI*, requiring no explicit prompting. Each time it is activated, the module generates a new response based on the latest voice transcript and the current sketch on the canvas. The transcript is also displayed and can be edited by the user, which immediately refreshes the AI Insights response to reflect the updated input.

On the back-end, the AI Insights module is powered by *Gemini 2.5 Flash* and customised to simulate the role of a design thinking expert. Following the Double Diamond framework [38], it guides users through the *Discover* and *Define* stages by identifying potential user needs, pain points, and framing design questions, before suggesting several exploratory directions to pursue. Two complementary prompt templates were developed to support different phases of the ideation process. When a user begins drawing on a new canvas, the system automatically triggers the *Kickoff Prompt* to initiate ideation; in subsequent interactions, as the user continues sketching or revising their transcript, the *Refine Prompt* is triggered to provide iterative feedback aligned with the evolving design concept. These prompts were iteratively tested to balance interpretability, creativity support, and brevity of response.

The final versions of the prompts are shown below:

> **Kickoff Prompt:** *"Act as a design thinking expert: based on the transcript and sketch canvas, identify what the user is trying to design, then—using*

---

[7] https://cloud.google.com/speech-to-text
[8] https://ai.google.dev/gemini-api/docs/models

the Double Diamond framework—guide them through Discover and Define by highlighting potential user needs, pain points, and framing questions, and finally offer 3 – 4 concise design directions in an encouraging and curious tone (around 100 words)."

Refine Prompt: *"Act as a design thinking collaborator: based on the updated transcript and sketch canvas, briefly summarise what the user is currently designing or refining, reflect their key idea in one or two sentences, suggest 1 – 2 small ways to expand or clarify it, and end with 1 – 2 open-ended questions to help further develop the concept in a supportive, conversational tone (around 80 – 100 words)."*

The second feature, **Multimodal AI Chat Interface** (Fig. 1d), facilitates open-ended conversations with a chatbot. Users may provide input either by typing text prompts or by utilising the iPad's integrated Voice Dictation functionality. In addition, the interface allows users to export selected regions of their sketch canvas into the chatbot as image-based inputs.

The chatbot supports two output modes: *Text Generation Mode* for verbal suggestions and *Image Generation Mode* for visual inspiration. In the *Text Generation Mode*, users can either submit only text input or combine their text prompt with a sketch, allowing the system to interpret both modalities but produce a text-only response. In the *Image Generation Mode*, users may similarly provide a text-only prompt or combine a text prompt with a freehand sketch, both of which will generate an image accompanied by a matching text description. The generated images can then be imported back into the canvas to serve as visual references or be integrated into the sketch, enabling users to freely incorporate AI-generated content as they iteratively refine their designs.

4.2   System Walkthrough

TALKSKETCH aims to support designers in early-stage ideation by combining freehand sketching, verbal thinking, and multimodal AI assistance. We illustrate its use through a walkthrough exemplar (Fig. 2) where a fictional user *Sky* is tasked with designing a household toaster. Her interaction follows a natural flow: sketching while speaking aloud, triggering the chatbot interface, reviewing automatically generated AI insights, and exploring further via multimodal interaction.

Sketching While Talking. *Sky* begins the design session by drawing a rough concept of a cube-shaped toaster with symbolic radial dials and a handle (see Fig. 1a). As she sketches, she verbalises her thoughts, *"I'm thinking of something bold and square, with a dial for heat control."* Her speech is recorded and transcribed in real time (see Fig. 1b), forming a synchronised verbal-visual trace of her ideation process.

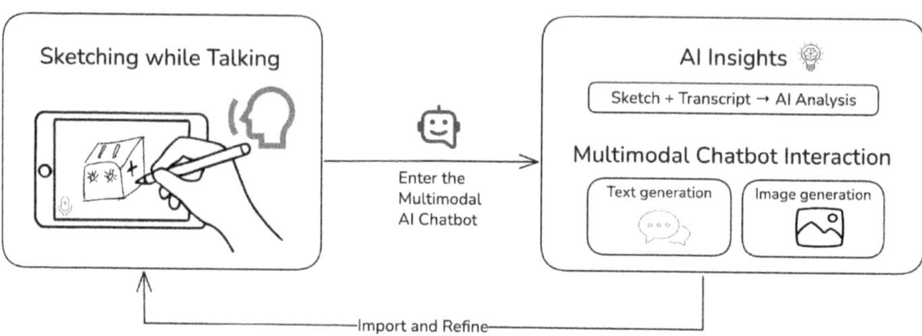

Fig. 2. The workflow of the TALKSKETCH system. The process starts with **Sketching with Talking**, where users draw freely on a tablet while voicing their ideas. These inputs are channelled into the **Multimodal AI Chatbot**, which generates AI Insights based on the user's sketch and transcript. Users then engage in exploration via **Multimodal Interaction**, with text or image generation to improve their design ideas. Finally, users can export AI-generated images back to the canvas for further sketching and refinement.

Entering the Chatbot and Viewing AI Insights. When *Sky* clicks *Generate with AI*, the system enters the chatbot interface (see Fig. 1d) and immediately displays an *AI Insight* (see Fig. 1c). This insight is automatically generated from her sketch and think-aloud transcript, offering concise design reflections based on the Double Diamond design thinking framework. The system suggests *emphasising geometric form* or *exploring tactile dials* as directions worth pursuing. Sky reads the insight and finds it helpful in framing her design direction. She realises she had forgotten to mention a few details aloud–such as her intention for the toaster to have a retractable cord–and decides to edit the transcript directly. After adding the missing information, she regenerates the *AI Insight* to see how the suggestions change in response to the fuller context.

Exploring via Multimodal Interaction. Sky then decides to follow up on the AI's suggestions. She first types into the chatbot input box: "Could you give me some ideas for drawing a novel toaster?" In *Text Generation Mode*, the chatbot responds with directions such as transparent exteriors and interactive touchscreens. Sky incorporates several of these into her sketch. To visualise the design, she switches to *Image Generation Mode*, prompting: *"Could you generate a realistic product based on my sketch?"* The system returns a refined visual that preserves key features from her drawing.

After a few rounds, Sky finds typing increasingly tedious and instead uses the built-in voice input feature. Her verbal prompt, *"What would a friendlier version look like?"*, is then transcribed and submitted automatically. The system responds with a new image featuring rounded corners, soft colours, and a smiling interface. Sky finds the result inspiring and chooses to export the AI-generated image back into the canvas, using it as a visual reference while continuing to sketch and refine her final design.

5   Potential Results

5.1   Enhancing Intent Expression and Interaction Naturalness

Building on prior research in multimodal CUIs [9,19,26], we expect that TALKS-KETCH will help designers communicate intent more fluidly by combining verbal and visual cues. While existing conversational AI systems require users to articulate ideas through discrete text prompts, TALKSKETCH allows designers to "think aloud" while drawing, preserving the spontaneity of natural dialogue [17,22,46]. This interaction form may reduce the cognitive effort involved in translating abstract ideas into prompts, a problem repeatedly identified in prompt-based creative tools [33,40]. By aligning the AI's interpretation with both speech and sketch input, users may experience the system as a more intuitive and responsive collaborator, one that feels closer to a design partner than a command-driven assistant. We therefore anticipate higher ratings of naturalness, communication clarity, and user control, reflecting an improved sense of mutual understanding between human and AI.

5.2   Supporting Creativity, Reflection, and Flow

Consistent with prior work on creativity-support systems [10,20,23,25,29,36], TALKSKETCH is designed to support early-stage ideation rather than polished production. We expect that integrating speech and sketch will enable designers to sustain creative flow by externalising thoughts continuously instead of interrupting the process to type or reformulate text. The AI Insight mechanism may further stimulate reflection by generating contextually relevant feedback from verbal and visual cues. Designers might pause to elaborate on their thinking, reinterpret sketches, or refine concepts based on AI suggestions, which echoes the dialogic creativity patterns observed in prior sketch-based systems [6,34]. This dynamic may lead to richer ideation traces and a stronger sense of co-evolution between human and AI ideas. Potential outcomes include higher perceived creativity support, increased exploratory behaviour, and a shift from command – response interaction to reflective conversation.

6   Limitations

This system has several limitations. First, because it depends on speech input, any transcription errors caused by background noise, unclear pronunciation, or the system mishearing words may lead to incorrect speech input. These mistakes may cause errors for the model to combine speech with sketches and to understand the user's design intent. Second, in some cases, users may prefer not to speak when they are sketching alone. In such cases, the system may need to rely only on sketches and user prompting in the chatbot to support their needs, reducing a layer of speech information. However, as early-stage sketches are often incomplete or ambiguous, combining them with short or minimal prompts may make it difficult for the system to understand user needs compared to with speech information. Third, the system currently interprets speech and sketch inputs as a single combined chunk within a period of time, which inevitably leads to some information loss. Different parts of a spoken description may refer to different regions in the sketch, yet the system cannot yet distinguish these finer-grained correspondences. As a result, important links between what is said and what is drawn may be missed, limiting the precision with which user intent is understood.

7   Conclusion and Future Work

This paper presented TALKSKETCH, a multimodal generative-AI sketching system that enables designers to ideate by sketching while speaking. Through a formative study with six designers, we identified key challenges in using existing GenAI chatbots for early-stage ideation, particularly the difficulty of translating evolving visual ideas into effective text prompts. To address these issues, TALKSKETCH integrates freehand drawing with real-time speech input, allowing users to externalise ideas more fluidly and engage in continuous dialogue with an embedded multimodal AI chatbot. By linking verbal and visual expression, TALKSKETCH demonstrates how conversational multimodal interfaces can support more natural and reflective design workflows.

Future work will involve a controlled user study to systematically evaluate how TALKSKETCH affects the naturalness of human – AI interaction and the perceived creativity of the design process. This next step aims to provide empirical evidence for the benefits of sketch-and-speech interaction in multimodal generative design tools. Beyond creativity support, it will also be valuable to explore how this interaction style can generalise to other settings, such as live demonstrations where rapid idea communication is essential, online classrooms where instructors sketch while explaining concepts, and collaborative design reviews where teams annotate evolving visuals. Examining these broader use cases may reveal additional opportunities for applying sketch-and-speech interaction as a more versatile interface paradigm.

References

1. Adler, A., Davis, R.: Speech and sketching for multimodal design. In: ACM SIGGRAPH 2007 Courses, pp. 14–es. SIGGRAPH '07, Association for Computing Machinery, New York, NY, USA (2007). https://doi.org/10.1145/1281500.1281525
2. Adobe Inc.: Adobe firefly: generative AI for creative workflows (2025). https://www.adobe.com/sensei/generative-ai/firefly.html
3. Angert, T., Suzara, M., Han, J., Pondoc, C., Subramonyam, H.: Spellburst: a node-based interface for exploratory creative coding with natural language prompts. In: Proceedings of the 36th Annual ACM Symposium on User Interface Software and Technology. UIST '23, Association for Computing Machinery, New York, NY, USA (2023). https://doi.org/10.1145/3586183.3606719

4. de Barcelos Silva, A., et al.: Intelligent personal assistants: a systematic literature review. Exp. Syst. Appl. **147**, 113193 (2020). https://doi.org/10.1016/j.eswa.2020.113193

5. Bolt, R.A.: put-that-there: Voice and gesture at the graphics interface. In: Proceedings of the 7th Annual Conference on Computer Graphics and Interactive Techniques. p. 262–270. SIGGRAPH '80, Association for Computing Machinery, New York, NY, USA (1980). https://doi.org/10.1145/800250.807503

6. Buxton, B.: Sketching user experiences: getting the design right and the right design. Elsevier, San Francisco, CA, USA (2010). https://doi.org/10.1016/b978-0-12-374037-3.x5043-3

7. Canva: Canva magic studio: AI-powered design tools (2025). https://www.canva.com/magic/

8. Cheng, Z., Chen, P., Song, W., Zhang, H., Li, Z., Sun, L.: An exploratory study on how ai awareness impacts human-ai design collaboration. In: Proceedings of the 30th International Conference on Intelligent User Interfaces, pp. 157–172. IUI '25, ACM, New York, NY, USA (2025). https://doi.org/10.1145/3708359.3712162

9. Cho, H., et al.: Persistent assistant: seamless everyday ai interactions via intent grounding and multimodal feedback. In: Proceedings of the 2025 CHI Conference on Human Factors in Computing Systems. pp. 1–19. CHI '25, ACM, New York, NY, USA (2025). https://doi.org/10.1145/3706598.3714317

10. Davis, R.L., et al.: Sketchai: A sketch-first approach to incorporating generative AI into fashion design. In: Proceedings of the Extended Abstracts of the CHI Conference on Human Factors in Computing Systems, pp. 1–7. CHI EA '25, ACM, New York, NY, USA (2025). https://doi.org/10.1145/3706599.3719782

11. Feuerriegel, S., Hartmann, J., Janiesch, C., Zschech, P.: Generative AI. Bus. Inf. Syst. Eng. **66**(1), 111–126 (2024). https://doi.org/10.1007/s12599-023-00834-7

12. Figma Inc.: Figma AI and FIGJAM AI features (2025). https://www.figma.com/ai/

13. Følstad, A., Brandtzæg, P.B.: Chatbots and the new world of HCI. Interactions **24**(4), 38–42 (2017). https://doi.org/10.1145/3085558

14. Fry, D.B.: The physics of speech. Cambridge University Press, Cambridge (1979). https://doi.org/10.1017/cbo9781139165747

15. Fui-Hoon Nah, F., Zheng, R., Cai, J., Siau, K., Chen, L.: Generative ai and chatgpt: applications, challenges, and AI-human collaboration. J. Inf. Technol. Case Appl. Res. **25**(3), 277–304 (2023). https://doi.org/10.1080/15228053.2023.2233814

16. Giunchi, D., Sztrajman, A., James, S., Steed, A.: Mixing modalities of 3D sketching and speech for interactive model retrieval in virtual reality. In: ACM International Conference on Interactive Media Experiences, pp. 144–155. IMX '21, ACM, New York, NY, USA (2021). https://doi.org/10.1145/3452918.3458806

17. He, Y., et al.: Enhancing intent understanding for ambiguous prompt: a human-machine co-adaption strategy (2025). https://arxiv.org/abs/2501.15167

18. Hedderich, M.A., Bazarova, N.N., Zou, W., Shim, R., Ma, X., Yang, Q.: A piece of theatre: investigating how teachers design LLM chatbots to assist adolescent cyberbullying education. In: Proceedings of the CHI Conference on Human Factors in Computing Systems, pp. 1–17. CHI '24, ACM, New York, NY, USA (2024). https://doi.org/10.1145/3613904.3642379

19. Hu, X., et al.: Gesprompt: liveraging co-speech gestures to augment LLM-based interaction in virtual reality. In: Proceedings of the 2025 ACM Designing Interactive Systems Conference, pp. 59–80. DIS '25, ACM, New York, NY, USA (2025). https://doi.org/10.1145/3715336.3735769

20. Kang, Y., Rao, J., Wang, W., Peng, B., Gao, S., Zhang, F.: Towards cartographic knowledge encoding with deep learning: a case study of building generalization. In: Proceedings of the AutoCarto, pp. 1–6 (2020)
21. Kim, J., et al.: A study on designer's mental process of information categorization in the early stages of design. In: Proceedings of the International Association of Societies of Design Research (IASDR) Conference, pp. 2401–2410. The International Association of Societies of Design Research (IASDR), Seoul, South Korea (2009)
22. Lan, G., et al.: Contextual integrity in LLMs via reasoning and reinforcement learning (2025). https://arxiv.org/abs/2506.04245
23. Lan, G., et al.: Mappo: maximum a posteriori preference optimization with prior knowledge (2025). https://arxiv.org/abs/2507.21183
24. Landay, J.A., Myers, B.A.: Interactive sketching for the early stages of user interface design. In: Proceedings of the SIGCHI Conference on Human Factors in Computing Systems - CHI '95, pp. 43–50. CHI '95, ACM Press, USA (1995). https://doi.org/10.1145/223904.223910
25. Lin, D.C.E., Kang, H.B., Martelaro, N., Kittur, A., Chen, Y.Y., Hong, M.K.: Inkspire: supporting design exploration with generative ai through analogical sketching. In: Proceedings of the 2025 CHI Conference on Human Factors in Computing Systems, pp. 1–18. CHI '25, ACM, New York, NY, USA (2025). https://doi.org/10.1145/3706598.3713397
26. Masson, D., Malacria, S., Casiez, G., Vogel, D.: Directgpt: a direct manipulation interface to interact with large language models. In: Proceedings of the CHI Conference on Human Factors in Computing Systems, pp. 1–16. CHI '24, ACM, New York, NY, USA (2024). https://doi.org/10.1145/3613904.3642462
27. McTear, M.F.: Spoken dialogue technology: enabling the conversational user interface. ACM Comput. Surv. (CSUR) **34**(1), 90–169 (2002). https://doi.org/10.1145/505282.505285
28. OpenAI: GPT-4 Technical Report (2023). https://doi.org/10.48550/ARXIV.2303.08774
29. Peng, X., Koch, J., Mackay, W.E.: Designprompt: using multimodal interaction for design exploration with generative AI. In: Proceedings of the 2024 ACM Designing Interactive Systems Conference, pp. 804–818. DIS '24, ACM, New York, NY, USA (2024). https://doi.org/10.1145/3643834.3661588
30. Purcell, A., Gero, J.: Drawings and the design process: a review of protocol studies in design and other disciplines and related research in cognitive psychology. Des. Stud. **19**(4), 389–430 (1998). https://doi.org/10.1016/s0142-694x(98)00015-5
31. Rosenberg, K.T., Kazi, R.H., Wei, L.Y., Xia, H., Perlin, K.: Drawtalking: building interactive worlds by sketching and speaking. In: Proceedings of the 37th Annual ACM Symposium on User Interface Software and Technology, pp. 1–25. UIST '24, ACM, New York, NY, USA (2024). https://doi.org/10.1145/3654777.3676334
32. Shaer, O., Cooper, A., Mokryn, O., Kun, A.L., Ben Shoshan, H.: AI-augmented brainwriting: Investigating the use of LLMs in group ideation. In: Proceedings of the CHI Conference on Human Factors in Computing Systems, pp. 1–17. CHI '24, ACM, New York, NY, USA (2024). https://doi.org/10.1145/3613904.3642414
33. Subramonyam, H., Pea, R., Pondoc, C., Agrawala, M., Seifert, C.: Bridging the gulf of envisioning: cognitive challenges in prompt based interactions with llms. In: Proceedings of the CHI Conference on Human Factors in Computing Systems, pp. 1–19. CHI '24, ACM, New York, NY, USA (2024). https://doi.org/10.1145/3613904.3642754

34. Suwa, M., Gero, J.S., Purcell, T.A.: The roles of sketches in early conceptual design processes, pp. 1043–1048. Routledge, Oxfordshire (2022). https://doi.org/10.4324/9781315782416-188

35. Tankelevitch, L., et al.: The metacognitive demands and opportunities of generative AI. In: Proceedings of the CHI Conference on Human Factors in Computing Systems, pp. 1–24. CHI '24, ACM, New York, NY, USA (2024). https://doi.org/10.1145/3613904.3642902

36. Tao, S., Liang, I., Peng, C., Wang, Z., Palani, S., Dow, S.P.: Designweaver: dimensional scaffolding for text-to-image product design. In: Proceedings of the 2025 CHI Conference on Human Factors in Computing Systems, pp. 1–26. CHI '25, ACM, New York, NY, USA (2025). https://doi.org/10.1145/3706598.3714211

37. Team, G.: Gemini 1.5: unlocking multimodal understanding across millions of tokens of context (2024). https://doi.org/10.48550/ARXIV.2403.05530

38. Tschimmel, K.: Design thinking as an effective toolkit for innovation. In: ISPIM conference proceedings, p. 1. The International Society for Professional Innovation Management (ISPIM), Unpublished, Barcelona, Spain (2012). https://doi.org/10.13140/2.1.2570.3361

39. Vinker, Y., Shaham, T.R., Zheng, K., Zhao, A., Fan, J.E., Torralba, A.: Sketchagent: language-driven sequential sketch generation. In: 2025 IEEE/CVF Conference on Computer Vision and Pattern Recognition (CVPR), pp. 23355–23368. IEEE, Nashville, TN, USA (2025). https://doi.org/10.1109/cvpr52734.2025.02175

40. Wang, J., et al.: Enhancing code LLMs with reinforcement learning in code generation: a survey (2025). https://arxiv.org/abs/2412.20367

41. Winograd, T.: Understanding natural language. Cogn. Psychol. **3**(1), 1–191 (1972). https://doi.org/10.1016/0010-0285(72)90002-3

42. Xu, S., Wei, Y., Zheng, P., Zhang, J., Yu, C.: Llm enabled generative collaborative design in a mixed reality environment. J. Manuf. Syst. **74**, 703–715 (2024). https://doi.org/10.1016/j.jmsy.2024.04.030

43. Yue, X., et al.: Mmmu: A massive multi-discipline multimodal understanding and reasoning benchmark for expert AGI. In: Proceedings of the IEEE/CVF Conference on Computer Vision and Pattern Recognition, pp. 9556–9567. IEEE, Seattle, WA, USA (2024). https://doi.org/10.1109/cvpr52733.2024.00913

44. Zhang, C., Wang, W., Pangaro, P., Martelaro, N., Byrne, D.: Generative image AI using design sketches as input: opportunities and challenges. In: Creativity and Cognition, pp. 254–261. C&C '23, ACM, New York, NY, USA (2023). https://doi.org/10.1145/3591196.3596820

45. Zhang, Z., Sun, B., An, P.: Breaking barriers or building dependency? Exploring team-llm collaboration in AI-infused classroom debate. In: Proceedings of the 2025 CHI Conference on Human Factors in Computing Systems, pp. 1–19. CHI '25, ACM, New York, NY, USA (2025). https://doi.org/10.1145/3706598.3713853

46. Zhao, P., et al.: Probabilistic contingent planning based on hierarchical task network for high-quality plans. Algorithms **18**(4) (2025). https://doi.org/10.3390/a18040214

47. Zhou, J., Myers-Dean, D., Gurari: Generating parts of objects for rapid prototyping. In: 2025 IEEE/CVF Conference on Computer Vision and Pattern Recognition (CVPR) Workshops (2025)

48. Çelen, A., et al.: I-Design: Personalized LLM Interior Designer, pp. 217–234. Springer Nature Switzerland, Berlin, Heidelberg (2024). https://doi.org/10.1007/978-3-031-92387-6_17

TradJockey: Live Remixing a Performance System for Traditional Music

Marco Amerotti[(✉)]

Mixed Reality Lab, School of Computer Science, University of Nottingham,
Nottingham, UK
marco.amerotti@nottingham.ac.uk

Abstract. This work presents an approach to interacting with
LOERIC, a music performance system for Irish Traditional Dance Music
(ITM) previously developed to be highly customisable and reactive in
real time. Using a commonly available MIDI controller, LOERIC can be
steered and fine-tuned to follow specific musical intentions and create
new performance possibilities. The potential for embodied, touch-driven
interaction, how it relates to previous research on LOERIC in terms of
autonomy and trust, and its creative potential are discussed, together
with future work and ethical considerations.

Keywords: Irish Traditional Dance Music · Performance System ·
Real-Time Interaction

1 Introduction

LOERIC is a rule-based, live and interactive music performance system within
the domain of Irish Traditional Dance Music (ITM), developed through practice-
led research [1]. At its core, LOERIC receives as input the basic melody for a
traditional tune (sometimes called "the bare bones" by practitioners) and is able
to interpret it by introducing rhythm, ornamentation, occasional polyphony,
dynamics, articulation and so on. The performance model has been iteratively
defined and refined using my own and my collaborators' practice, books and
other academic works (*e.g.* [12,13]), and expert knowledge elicited through various interactions with traditional musicians. The performance of ITM is centred
on playing traditional tunes that are commonly distinguished in various musical
forms or dances – reels, jigs, hornpipes, slides, polkas, *etc.* – usually multiple
times, on different traditional instruments (*e.g.* fiddles, flutes, accordions, con-
certinas, guitars, banjos, the uilleann pipes, *etc.*), both solo and in groups; the
latter constitutes a very important part of the practice through what is known
as "sessions", where multiple musicians gather to play tunes in heterophony, with
limited accompaniment mostly provided by guitars, bouzoukis and citterns.

As a result, from the start, LOERIC was designed to be able to interact
in real time with a co-musician: interaction with it is based on a measure of

© The Author(s), under exclusive license to Springer Nature Switzerland AG 2026
K. Woodward et al. (Eds.): CLIP 2026, CCIS 2865, pp. 98–106, 2026.
https://doi.org/10.1007/978-3-032-16893-1_7

"performance intensity" that tries to loosely encode how "intensely" its partner is playing, and on configuration files that specify how to respond. So far, we have experimented with connecting this measure with the loudness of the co-musician, or an expression pedal/footswitch (more details are available in [1–3]).

While this might seem (and probably is) a very reductive way to model musical interaction, it has yielded interesting results; at the same time, using only audio as an interaction modality both limits the amount of control available to the co-musician and possibly inhibits, or at least makes more difficult, an embodied interaction with the system, especially important in the musical domain [10].

In what follows, I explore interaction with LOERIC through a MIDI mixer interface that allows real-time, fine-grained control of the system; I later present a preliminary evaluation while performing with the system and discuss the potential for embodied, touch-driven interaction, how it relates with previous research on LOERIC in terms of autonomy and trust, and its creative potential. Finally, future work and ethical concerns are discussed.

2   Interaction in LOERIC

I now present a technical account of LOERIC, focusing on how interaction is achieved; further details on the overall system can be found in [1].

The system is entirely based on MIDI, both for output (sound generation is delegated to an external synthesiser) and input (through MIDI CC messages). It is also highly customisable in the vast majority of its parameters through extensive configuration files.

As mentioned above, the performance model underlying LOERIC is obtained through its developers' practice and expert knowledge from both the academic discourse on ITM and practitioners. The main device for translating this knowledge in a machine-readable form is through note-wise control functions, which are used to specify a variety of attributes for each note in the source score, *e.g.* how soft or loud it is, how probable it is it would be ornamented, how likely the note is to be accompanied by a drone, if it should be played staccato or legato, and so on. An example is shown in Fig. 1.

Similarly, an interacting musician can send their own performance intensity – which can be computed from *e.g.* the loudness of their signal, or the value output by a fader or expression pedal – and LOERIC will interpolate between this signal and its control functions using Eq. 1:

$$h \cdot u + (1 - h) \cdot c \tag{1}$$

where u is the value of the user signal, c is LOERIC's original contour value, and h corresponds to the *human impact* parameter, *i.e.* the weight of the user signal over LOERIC's contours. u, c and h are in the interval $[0, 1]$; for u and c, 0 corresponds to "low intensity" and 1 to "high intensity", whereas $h = 0$ corresponds to full system autonomy (*i.e.* the system does not consider the user signal) and $h = 1$ to full user control on the system. Different contours can have

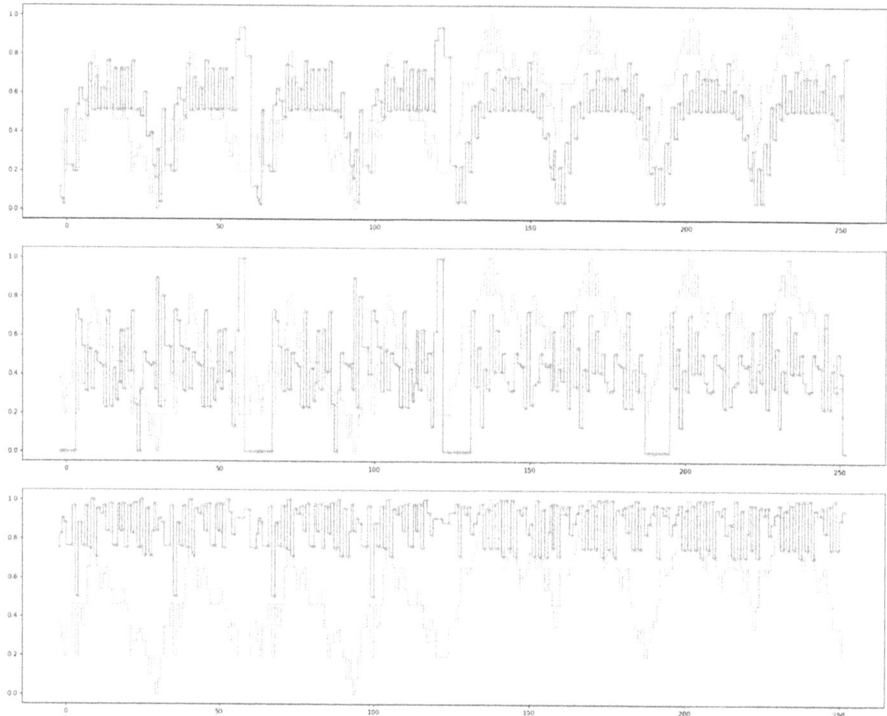

Fig. 1. Control functions generated by LOERIC for the hornpipe "The Home Ruler". From the top, dynamics, ornamentation, and legato. The abscissa represents performance time in eighth notes, the ordinate intensity in the range $[0, 1]$. The pitch contour of the tune is dotted in blue; the control functions are solid in orange.

different human impact values, and the parameter can be specified at program start or itself controlled in real time.

In this way, the system matches the user's signal to the extent specified by h; however, it can also "oppose" it – signalled by a negative value of human impact – using the following formula (Eq. 2):

$$|h| \cdot u + (1 - |h|) \cdot (1 - c) \tag{2}$$

The resulting effect is that the user's signal steers LOERIC control functions to be lower or higher than originally computed, and this can be exploited to either match the user's behaviour (*e.g.* "play soft when I play soft") or invert it (*e.g.* allowing one to take the lead over another and vice-versa).

As mentioned earlier, the system allows for fine-grained customisation of how each control function is controlled by different signals through JSON configuration files, *e.g.*, as in this snippet (Fig. 2):

which translates to the following:

– low system autonomy for legato, with inverted control, computed using Eq. 2;

```
"contours": {
    "legato": { "human_impact_scale": -0.75 },
    "ornament": { "human_impact_scale": 1 },
    "tempo": { "human_impact_scale": 1 }
},
"control_2_contour": {
    "ornaments": {
        "control": 77,
        "contours": [ "ornament_intensity", "legato_intensity" ]
    },
    "tempo": {
        "control": 78,
        "contours": [ "tempo_intensity" ]
    }
}
```

Fig. 2. Excerpt of a configuration file for interacting with LOERIC.

- no system autonomy for ornamentation, with normal control, using Eq. 1;
- no system autonomy for tempo, normal control, using Eq. 1;
- control both ornamentation and legato through MIDI CC 77;
- control tempo through MIDI CC 78.

With this configuration, LOERIC would introduce ornaments and play staccato when CC 77 is high, and play less elaborately and legato otherwise, and it would play slower or faster depending on how low or high the value of CC 78 is.

3   The TradJockey Setup

Being based on MIDI, LOERIC offers out-of-the-box compatibility with standard music production software (*e.g.* DAWs) and MIDI controllers. One powerful aspect of using the latter is that many of them are affordable, familiar to musicians and performers, and often already present in their workflow; moreover, they are not susceptible to ambient noises, unlike the microphone interaction setup, and they allow dialling in specific values with reasonable accuracy for different control functions. In this work, I used the Novation Launch Control XL mixer, which provides 8 faders and 24 knobs, together with other utility buttons.

   I originally obtained this controller for development purposes, with the idea of feeding specific control values to LOERIC and quickly changing its parameters to ensure the system was working as planned and to debug it. In my first iterations, I set it up as follows:

- faders 1 and 2: dynamics intensity and dynamics human impact;
- faders 3 and 4: ornament intensity and ornament human impact;
- faders 5 and 6: tempo intensity and tempo human impact.

This allowed me to rapidly and precisely change (1) what intensity LOERIC was fed, and (2) how much it would listen, separately for each attribute. This proved to work well in the development process, and I soon started experimenting with different setups depending on what needed testing.

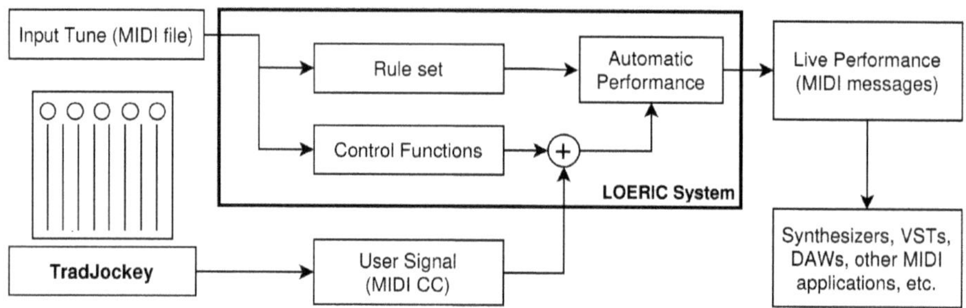

Fig. 3. The TradJockey and LOERIC setup.

After having become acquainted with this way of interaction, I realised its potential as a way of demoing the system for other researchers or collaborating musicians. The interface allowed me to control multiple parameters at the same time, and also offered a visual feedback of what was happening, both for the observers and myself (LOERIC currently lacks any visual representation, apart from what it prints on its terminal window). It also made it easy to selectively showcase its growing array of features without having to repeatedly stop, configure and restart the system every time. Communicating with LOERIC through its standard interaction mechanisms, the whole system acts in real time with no delay: LOERIC updates its control functions as soon as it receives a control change message using Eq. 1 or Eq. 2, which are trivial to compute. This demo setup eventually became the TradJockey configuration, which maps each fader to the following parameters, in order:

1. ornament intensity;
2. errors intensity;
3. drones intensity;
4. legato intensity;
5. dynamics intensity;
6. swing intensity, from straight to what the particular tune type requires;
7. tempo intensity, with a deviation of 50 bpm around the original tempo.

For each control function, the human impact is set to 1, except for swing.[1] A diagram of this setup is shown in Fig. 3.

---

[1] In LOERIC, swing is often connected to overall tempo, so that faster tempi correspond to straighter playing: as such, for swing, lower intensities correspond to greater swing and vice-versa. To preserve compatibility with other configurations, and also have an intuitive slider from "straight" to "swung", the human impact is set to –1, inverting the relationship.

Table 1. The different stages of the test performance and the approximate values of TradJockey's parameters.

Stage	Ornament	Errors	Drones	Legato	Dynamics	Swing	Tempo
Start	0.0	0.0	0.0	0.0	0.0	0.0	0.0
Drones	0.0	0.0	1.0	1.0	1.0	0.0	0.1
Traditional	0.8	0.0	0.3	0.8	1.0	0.6	0.7
Glitch	0.8	1.0	0.0	0.8	1.0	0.6	0.7
Errors	1.0	1.0	0.0	0.1	1.0	0.1	0.0

4 Preliminary Evaluation

I now examine a performance setup enabled by this system, allowing one to "remix" a tune live, radically changing how it sounds throughout different sections. I chose the tune "The Sailor's Cravat" and experimented with different settings, using a saw synthesiser for sound generation. An audio recording of my interaction is provided[2], and described in what follows. Table 1 summarises the different stages of the performance and the respective fader settings.

The system starts with all parameters set to a middle level of intensity, which prompts me to "tame it" by setting all faders to 0 (Start). This creates a first slow-tempo, staccato, quiet and monophonic moment. I then proceed to gradually introduce drones, increase the tempo and legato, until LOERIC is playing full-legato, with abundant held drones and at a consistent tempo (Drones). This can later morph into a more traditional-sounding rendition by limiting the use of drones and introducing swing and ornamentation (Traditional). So far, the system has been playing in a very melodic and recognisable way, so I decide to "glitch" it: I suddenly introduce errors and turn off the drones, making the tune still recognisable, but hidden behind the frequent "wrong notes" (Glitch). By forcing LOERIC to play very staccato, reducing the tempo and the amount of swing, the tune starts sounding more like a series of disconnected random pitches, though emerging from the "noise" at times (Errors). By this time, LOERIC stopped, having met the number of repetitions specified at the start.

Being used to interacting with LOERIC using a musical instrument, the TradJockey system forced me into another kind of musical interaction: I did not need to focus contemporarily on the system and my own playing, and that shifted my attention to what LOERIC was doing, and how I wished to change that; together with eliminating autonomy from the system (setting all human impact values to 1 and −1), this prompted me to start *controlling* LOERIC rather than *dialoguing* with it, which was how I usually interacted with the system in my own practice; finally, I could create very different sounding configurations in real time and try to obtain new musicalities that, while already possible in

---

[2] See this website: https://www.nottingham.ac.uk/research/groups/mixedrealitylab/people/marco.amerotti.

the system's configuration space, I had not yet encountered, or I would have needed to put together over multiple iterations. These points are discussed in the following section.

5   Discussion

When using audio interaction, LOERIC's parameters are entangled on a single, "fuzzy" interaction channel and only become apparent by carefully listening to the system; the system outlined above instead materialises these parameters into faders that provide a physical interface to the system. The two immediate consequences are, first, the adoption of a different role by the human musician when interacting with LOERIC – from co-musician to conductor, or DJ perhaps – and second, a new possibility for embodiment deriving from the touch-driven nature of the interaction and the physical mobility gained from not using a musical instrument to play with LOERIC. Building on [6], this kind of interaction with LOERIC can be considered a form of controllerism, where the tactile immediacy of interfaces both makes the digital software physical and enables the user to embody their performance without being mere "button pushers" (*ibid.*). Still following D'Errico, we could frame this interaction as musical *play*: the controller externalises the rules of the music/game and of the digital system itself, and, by physically mapping these, it prompts the user to develop and internalise specific embodied musical techniques.

Expanding on [3], this switch of perspective also impacts how the system is perceived in terms of autonomy and trust: in my experience, from the reduced autonomy ascribed to the system I could see LOERIC as more reliable when it came to following my intentions; at the same time, this shifts the weight of carrying a performance entirely on the human and makes the system appear less trustworthy. For example, the TradJockey system could suddenly stop responding as planned, and the performance would effectively fail; instead, a performance setting not focused on finely controlling LOERIC could still allow for a meaningful interaction. In that case, the machine – being a mere executor of the human's intentions – would not share the blame for a poor performance, which would fall onto its human partner entirely.

Another interesting aspect of the experience is how easily and quickly the tune could be "remixed", both towards a conventional sound, reminiscent of what one could hear in traditional practice, and a completely alien territory that makes the tune unrecognisable. This had already been explored in [3], setting up LOERIC so that the tune would emerge from a "stream of errors" whenever the human musician started playing, but this required a bespoke configuration file for that setting only; TradJockey can now morph seamlessly between different setups in real time, and with finer control of the attributes involved. In particular, the practices of glitching [11] and circuit bending [7] are useful ways to charting a creative space. For example, considering Boden's famous typisation [4], TradJockey can be seen as an example of combinatorial creativity, shuffling the sliders around to obtain unseen combinations; it can be framed within exploratory creativity when trying to push LOERIC from a known musicality to a new one, tweaking specific aspects; and it can also act as a transformational system in the design of the interface itself, that fuses traditionally understood parameters of ITM practice, such as ornamentation [9], together with unusual ones, such as "errors", and brings them together as the axes of a new conceptual space.

6   Conclusion

In this work, I presented a way of interacting with LOERIC, a rule-based and real-time performance system for ITM, using a mixer-like MIDI controller interface. Compared to other interaction modalities, the TradJockey system outlined here has the advantage of providing (1) a physical interface to the otherwise abstract, software-only system, and (2) establishing new possibilities for performing with the system, shifting the paradigm from interacting with an AI co-musician to controlling it to obtain specific sonorities and musical moments in a performance. The system acts fully in real time as the underlying operations are computationally inexpensive. A preliminary evaluation informally explored a performance possibility; I later discussed how TradJockey relates to previous research on LOERIC, how it can be used to power a touch-driven, embodied interaction with the system, as well as how it can foster creativity when experimenting with new musical aesthetics.

Future work will consider deploying this interface in a performance setting and testing different configurations and the kinds of interactions they can power. An interesting possibility would be to bring this system back to the practice of ITM, where it could, for example, be used in the emerging practice of "triscos" (traditional music discos, see [5]). It will be vital to engage with the community to identify possible applications or issues connected with the use of the system.

From an ethical standpoint, research with LOERIC needs to consider many important aspects of dealing with traditional practice: for example, how can we obtain consensus to carry out this kind of research from a community as wide and diverse as the one around ITM? How do we ensure that our research does not impact the tradition in a bad way, and what is a bad way of impacting the tradition? These, and many other questions, are fundamental to this kind of work and need to guide the research and development process. While the TradJockey system *per se* as an interaction paradigm does not explicitly pose any threat to traditional practice, its application and future developments might. To this end, I agree with Kanhov et al.'s recommendations [8]: researchers need to embrace interdisciplinary practice outside the domain of AI development, engage with communities of practice, and prioritise ethics in the research work.

Disclosure of Interests. The author has no competing interests to declare that are relevant to the content of this article.

References

1. Amerotti, M., Benford, S., Sturm, B.L.T., Vear, C.: A live performance rule system informed by irish traditional dance music. In: Ystad, S., Kronland-Martinet, R., Kitahara, T., Hirata, K., Aramaki, M. (eds.) Music and Sound Generation in the AI Era, pp. 127–139. Springer, Cham (2026). https://doi.org/10.1007/978-3-032-02042-0_9
2. Amerotti, M., Sturm, B.L.T., Benford, S., Maruri-Aguilar, H., Vear, C.: Evaluation of an interactive music performance system in the context of Irish traditional dance music. In: Bin, S.M.A., Reed, C.N. (eds.) Proceedings of the International Conference on New Interfaces for Musical Expression, pp. 149–153. Utrecht, Netherlands (2024). https://doi.org/10.5281/zenodo.13904812, http://nime.org/proceedings/2024/nime2024_23.pdf
3. Benford, S., Amerotti, M., Sturm, B.L.T., Martinez Avila, J.: Negotiating autonomy and trust when performing with an ai musician. In: Proceedings of the Second International Symposium on Trustworthy Autonomous Systems, pp. 1–10 (2024)
4. Boden, M.A.: The creative mind: myths & mechanisms. Basic Books (1991). https://api.semanticscholar.org/CorpusID:143261160
5. Cotter, P.: Carnage at the trisco: an ethnographic account of the trad disco at fleadh cheoil na héireann. Ethnomusicol. Ireland **8**, 62–84 (2022)
6. D'Errico, M.: Controller cultures. In: Push: Software Design and the Cultural Politics of Music Production. Oxford University Press (2022).https://doi.org/10.1093/oso/9780190943301.003.0005, https://doi.org/10.1093/oso/9780190943301.003.0005
7. Ghazala, Q.R.: Circuit-bending and living instruments. In: Sound Inventions, pp. 190–201. Focal Press (2021)
8. Kanhov, E., Kaila, A.K., Sturm, B.L.T.: Innovation, data colonialism and ethics: critical reflections on the impacts of ai on Irish traditional music. J. New Music Res. **53**(1–2), 47–63 (2024)
9. Keegan, N.: The parameters of style in Irish traditional music. Inbhearr: J. Irish Music Dance. **1**(1) (2010)
10. Leman, M., Maes, P.J., Nijs, L., Van Dyck, E.: What is embodied music cognition? In: Bader, R. (ed.) Springer Handbook of Systematic Musicology, pp. 747–760. Springer, Berlin, Heidelberg (2018).https://doi.org/10.1007/978-3-662-55004-5_34
11. Salah Eldin, O.: The aesthetics of imperfection; glitch art in three-dimension forms as a creative design tool. Int. Design J. **9**(3), 363–371 (2019)
12. Tourish, M.: In Process and Practice: The Development of an Archive of Explicit Stylistic Data for Irish Traditional Instrumental Music. Ph.D. thesis, Dublin Institute of Technology (2013). https://api.semanticscholar.org/CorpusID:62887196
13. Ó Canainn, T.: Traditional Music in Ireland. Routledge and Kegan Paul Ltd. (1978)

EVLM: Self-reflective Multimodal Reasoning and KTO Alignment for Cross-Dimensional Visual Editing

Umar Khalid[1(✉)], Kashif Munir[1(✉)], Hasan Iqbal[2], Azib Farooq[3], Jing Hua[2], Nazanin Rahnavard[4], Chen Chen[4], Victor Zhu[1], and Zhengping Ji[1]

[1] Axon, Scottsdale, USA
{ukhalid,kmunir,vzhu,zji}@axon.com
[2] Wayne State University, Detroit, USA
jinghua@wayne.edu
[3] Miami University, Oxford, USA
[4] University of Central Florida, Orlando, USA
{nazanin.rahnavard,chen.chen}@crcv.ucf.edu

Abstract. Editing complex visual content from ambiguous or partially specified instructions remains a core challenge in vision–language modeling. Existing models can contextualize content but often fail to infer the **underlying intent** within a reference image or scene, leading to inconsistent or misaligned edits. We introduce the Editing Vision–Language Model (EVLM), a system that interprets ambiguous instructions in conjunction with reference visuals to produce precise, context-aware editing prompts. EVLM's key innovation is a reflective reasoning framework that translates subjective user intent into structured, actionable outputs by aligning with human-rated rationales through Reflection-Aware KL-Divergence Target Optimization (RKTO). By combining Chain-of-Thought (CoT) reasoning with RKTO alignment, EVLM captures fine-grained editing preferences without relying on binary supervision. Trained on a dataset of 30,000 CoT examples with human-annotated rationale quality, EVLM achieves substantial gains in alignment with human intent. Experiments across image, video, 3D, and 4D editing tasks show that EVLM generates coherent and high-quality instructions, providing a scalable foundation for multimodal editing and reasoning.

1 Introduction

Recent advances in text-to-image (T2I) diffusion models have enabled free-form natural language to be transformed into photorealistic imagery with striking fidelity [16,36,37]. Building on this progress, instruction-based editors—*"modify this image according to that sentence"*—have become a natural interface for visual content creation [3,19,61]. However, as editing tasks become more open-ended and multimodal—combining vague language with incomplete visual cues—current systems often fail to interpret user intent. This raises a central challenge for multimodal reasoning: *can a model reason through ambiguity, reconciling partial textual hints with reference visuals to infer the user's intended edit?*

© The Author(s), under exclusive license to Springer Nature Switzerland AG 2026
K. Woodward et al. (Eds.): CLIP 2026, CCIS 2865, pp. 107–132, 2026.
https://doi.org/10.1007/978-3-032-16893-1_8

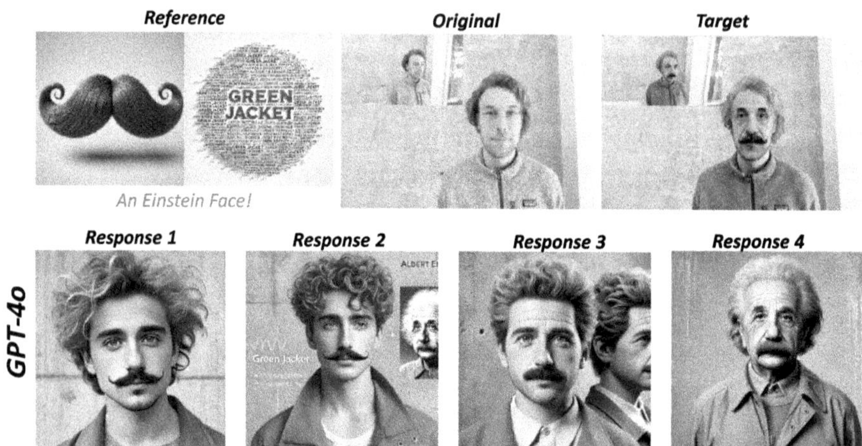

Fig. 1. Reference image and prompt for the 3D editing task: "An Einstein Face!" The reference includes an image with a mustache and the image-with-text "Green Jacket." These were provided to GPT-4o, along with supporting prompts (details in *supplementary*), to guide the generation of accurate editing instructions. GPT-4o encountered challenges integrating textual, visual, and OCR information to produce coherent instructions. Despite multiple attempts, DALL-E 3 guided by GPT-4o was unable to generate the desired edited image that fully aligns with the ***reference intent.***

Motivation. Prompt-refinement pipelines that attach a large language model to a diffusion decoder [12,62] perform well when instructions are explicit but lack *reflective reasoning.* Given an instruction such as *"Give it an Einstein face!"* with only weak visual hints (Fig. 1), these systems cannot justify *why* a specific region —such as the jacket—should inherit a pattern or texture. Two factors contribute to this limitation: (i) existing datasets contain only terse text–edit pairs, providing no supervision for reasoning, and (ii) preference optimization with PPO [39] captures only coarse binary rewards, which are unsuited for subjective, multi-solution editing tasks where subtle human preferences matter.

We introduce the **Editing Vision–Language Model (EVLM)**, a multimodal reasoning framework that interprets ambiguous editing instructions by combining textual, visual, and spatial cues. EVLM ingests diverse references—such as images, video clips, depth maps, or text—and outputs concise, disambiguated instructions together with target masks or object indices suitable for downstream visual editors.

Training proceeds in two complementary stages: (1) construction of the REFLECTIVE-EDIT dataset of 30k multimodal examples, where GPT-4o generates chain-of-thought rationales that are rated by human annotators as *desired* or *non-desired*; and (2) alternating phases of *Reflective Supervised Fine-Tuning* (SFT) and **Reflection-Aware KL-Divergence Target Optimization (RKTO)**, which align both the final instructions and the reflective reasoning process with human preferences. Together, these components enable EVLM

Fig. 2. EVLM enables editing across 2D, 3D, and 4D tasks. Given a reference image, video, or text instruction, EVLM generates precise and context-aware editing transformations. Examples include color and style modifications in 2D and 3D, and texture or dynamic edits in 4D scenarios. These results highlight EVLM's multimodal understanding of spatial, temporal, and semantic cues for complex visual editing.

not only to imitate editing instructions but also to reason reflectively about user intent with interpretable internal logic as illustrated in Fig. 2. Our main contributions are:

1. **EVLM**, a vision–language model capable of reflective multimodal reasoning for context-aware and interpretable editing across image, video, 3D, and 4D domains.
2. **REFLECTIVE-EDIT**, a 30k-example chain-of-thought dataset with human preference annotations designed to teach reflective reasoning for editing tasks.
3. **RKTO**, a preference-alignment framework that extends KL-divergence target optimization to jointly align instruction effectiveness and reflection quality, providing richer and more stable feedback than PPO-based methods.

2   Related Work

Reflection and Alignment in Multimodal Models. Recent work explores reflection in language and vision-language models to enable post-hoc self-correction and alignment with human intent. Methods use either external feedback (*e.g.*, execution traces, expert critiques) [4, 42] or internal self-evaluation [24, 29, 51], though reliability remains task-dependent [17]. Parallel efforts in vision-language models apply chain-of-thought reasoning to domains such as math [27, 48], scientific QA [28], and chart understanding [60]. Preference-alignment approaches like DPO [34, 45] and PPO [58] guide model fine-tuning, while iterative DPO [35, 46]

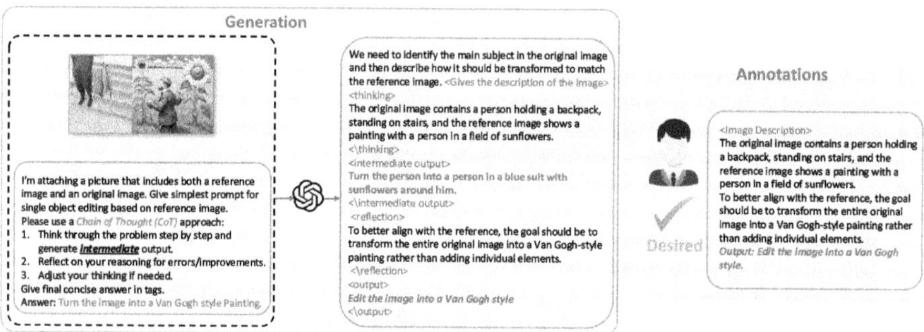

Fig. 3. Overview of our data preparation pipeline. Given a reference and target image, GPT-4o produces a structured chain-of-thought rationale through initial, intermediate, and reflective reasoning. Only the reflective and final outputs are used to construct RKTO training data, with human annotators providing "desired" labels when reasoning aligns with intended edits.

improves step-by-step reasoning. More recently, KTO [11] aligns model outputs to a soft reference distribution via KL-divergence, effectively modeling nuanced human preferences for subjective generation tasks such as visual editing (Fig. 3).

Diffusion-Based Editing Across Dimensions. Diffusion-based models enable text-driven editing across modalities, spanning 2D [3,15,32,38,47], 3D [9,13,18], and 4D [40,65] domains. Extensions to videos include Tune-A-Video [53], Make-A-Video [44], and MagicVideo [63], which leverage spatio-temporal attention to maintain consistency. Prompt-level control methods such as Prompt-to-Prompt [15] and Plug-and-Play [47] refine local edits, while 3D and 4D variants adapt text-to-image priors (e.g., IP2P) for NeRFs and dynamic scenes. Our work builds on these foundations by integrating reflective reasoning and alignment into the diffusion pipeline, yielding flexible editing across 2D, 3D, and 4D modalities.

3 Approach

The Editing Vision–Language Model (EVLM) converts multimodal editing intent (images, video, and text) into concise, interpretable editing instructions paired with spatial masks. Training proceeds in three stages: (1) construction of a REFLECTIVE-EDIT dataset, (2) supervised fine-tuning (SFT) of a Qwen2-VL-7B backbone to learn structured chain-of-thought (CoT) traces, and (3) Reflection-aware KL-Divergence Target Optimization (RKTO), which aligns both the generated instructions and the model's reflective reasoning with human preferences.

Notations. Let $x = (\mathcal{V}, u)$ denote the multimodal input, where $\mathcal{V}$ is the visual context and u the textual prompt. Let $\rho_\phi(\cdot \mid x)$ be the EVLM conditional distribution with parameters ϕ, $\rho_{\mathrm{ref}}(\cdot \mid x)$ the SFT snapshot (reference policy), and $\rho_{\text{pref}}(\cdot \mid x)$ the empirical human-preferred distribution induced by annotator labels. We write $\hat{y}$ for model-generated instruction tokens (decoded sample), y for reference instruction tokens, r_{refl} for the <reflection> segment of the CoT, $\hat{m}$ for the decoded discrete mask (from mask tokens), and m_{ref} for a reference mask when available. Cosine similarities are rescaled to $[0,1]$ via $\widetilde{\cos}(a,b) = (1+\cos(a,b))/2$. We use $\text{IoU}(\hat{m}, m_{\text{ref}}) = \frac{|\hat{m} \cap m_{\text{ref}}|}{|\hat{m} \cup m_{\text{ref}}|}$, and the importance-weight function $w(s) = \text{clip}(\text{softplus}(s), 0, w_{\max})$ with $\text{softplus}(s) = \log(1 + e^s)$. Let $e(\cdot)$ denote the Qwen2-VL text encoder.

3.1 REFLECTIVE-EDIT Dataset

We construct REFLECTIVE-EDIT with $\sim$30,000 multimodal examples. Each example contains x, one or more reference items (image/video/text), and a GPT-4o-generated CoT trace segmented into <thinking>, <intermediate>, <reflection>, and <output> sections. Human annotators mark traces as *desired* or *non-desired* and provide graded preference supervision for instruction quality and reflection quality, yielding ρ_{pref}.

3.2 Supervised Fine-Tuning (SFT)

EVLM first learns to reproduce teacher CoT traces via teacher forcing. For $(\mathcal{V}, u, y_{1:T})$ with optional mask tokens producing $\hat{m}$, the SFT objective is

$$\mathcal{L}_{\text{SFT}} = -\sum_{t=1}^{T} \log \rho_\phi(y_t \mid y_{<t}, u, \mathcal{V}), \tag{1}$$

which stabilizes token-level generation and defines the snapshot ρ_{ref} used as the baseline policy for alignment.

3.3 Reflection-Aware KTO (RKTO)

We extend KTO with a reflection-quality term so that EVLM aligns its instructions *and* its reflective reasoning to human preferences. For a preference tuple $(x, y_{\text{pref}}, m_{\text{ref}})$, we minimize

$$\mathcal{L}_{\text{RKTO}} = \mathbb{E}\big[w(s_\phi - \eta_0)\, R_{\text{eff}}(\hat{y}, \hat{m}; y_{\text{pref}}, m_{\text{ref}}) + \lambda_{\text{ref}}\, R_{\text{reflect}}(r_{\text{refl}})\big], \tag{2}$$

with log-ratio statistic and baseline

$$s_\phi = \log\frac{\rho_\phi(y_{\text{pref}} \mid x)}{\rho_{\text{ref}}(y_{\text{pref}} \mid x)}, \qquad \eta_0 = \text{KL}\big(\rho_\phi(\cdot \mid x) \,\|\, \rho_{\text{ref}}(\cdot \mid x)\big). \tag{3}$$

Instruction Effectiveness. When a reference mask is available,

$$R_{\text{eff}}(\hat{y}, \hat{m}; y_{\text{pref}}, m_{\text{ref}}) = \alpha\, \widetilde{\cos}\big(e(\hat{y}), e(y_{\text{pref}})\big) + (1-\alpha)\, \text{IoU}(\hat{m}, m_{\text{ref}}), \tag{4}$$

where $\alpha \in [0,1]$. Because IoU is non-differentiable for discrete masks, we use REINFORCE with a per-batch mean baseline b_{IoU}.

Reflection Reward. We encourage concise and semantically consistent reflection using

$$R_{\text{reflect}}(r_{\text{refl}}) = \beta_1 \, \widetilde{\cos}\big(e(r_{\text{refl}}), e(y_{\text{pref}})\big) + \beta_2 \, \exp\big(-\gamma \, \text{len}(r_{\text{refl}})\big)$$
$$+ \, \beta_3 \big(1 - \text{KL}\big(p_{\text{int}} \, \| \, p_{\text{refl}}\big)\big), \tag{5}$$

where p_{int} and p_{refl} are token distributions for the `<intermediate>` and `<reflection>` segments, $\text{len}(\cdot)$ is the token length of the reflection, $\beta_k \geq 0$ and $\sum_k \beta_k = 1$, and $\lambda_{\text{ref}} \geq 0$. We optimize $\mathcal{L}_{\text{reflect}} = 1 - R_{\text{reflect}}$ jointly with Eq. (2).

3.4   Batched Objective and Gradient Estimator

For a mini-batch $\{(x_i, y_{\text{pref}}^{(i)}, m_{\text{ref}}^{(i)})\}_{i=1}^{B}$, we use variance-reduced statistics

$$\hat{s}_\phi^{(i)} = \log \frac{\rho_\phi\big(y_{\text{pref}}^{(i)} \mid x_i\big)}{\rho_{\text{ref}}\big(y_{\text{pref}}^{(i)} \mid x_i\big)}, \quad \hat{\eta}_0 = \max\left(0, \frac{1}{B(B-1)} \sum_{i \neq j} \log \frac{\rho_\phi\big(y_{\text{pref}}^{(j)} \mid x_i\big)}{\rho_{\text{ref}}\big(y_{\text{pref}}^{(j)} \mid x_i\big)}\right), \tag{6}$$

and minimize the empirical loss

$$\widehat{\mathcal{L}}_{\text{RKTO}} = \frac{1}{B} \sum_{i=1}^{B} \left[w\big(\hat{s}_\phi^{(i)} - \hat{\eta}_0\big) R_{\text{eff}}^{(i)} + \lambda_{\text{ref}} R_{\text{reflect}}^{(i)} \right]. \tag{7}$$

Let

$$c_i = w\big(\hat{s}_\phi^{(i)} - \hat{\eta}_0\big), \qquad d_i = c_i \, (1 - \alpha) \big(\text{IoU}^{(i)} - b_{\text{IoU}}\big),$$

with b_{IoU} the per-batch mean IoU baseline. The gradient estimator used for updates is

$$\nabla_\phi \widehat{\mathcal{L}}_{\text{RKTO}} \approx \frac{1}{B} \sum_{i=1}^{B} c_i \, R_{\text{eff}}^{(i)} \, \nabla_\phi \log \rho_\phi\big(y_{\text{pref}}^{(i)} \mid x^{(i)}\big)$$
$$+ \, \lambda_{\text{ref}} \nabla_\phi \mathcal{L}_{\text{reflect}} \tag{8}$$
$$+ \, \frac{1}{B} \sum_{i=1}^{B} d_i \, \nabla_\phi \log \rho_\phi\big(\hat{m}^{(i)} \mid x^{(i)}\big).$$

Variance is reduced via importance-weight clipping ($w \in [0, w_{\max}]$), reward centering, smaller RKTO learning rates than SFT, optional averaging of multiple mask samples, and gradient clipping.

3.5   Training Algorithm and Optimization

We optimize EVLM in alternating *SFT* and *RKTO* phases (Algorithm 1).

SFT Phase. Minimize Eq. (1) with teacher forcing to learn structured CoT traces and a stable baseline policy. We periodically snapshot the current model as the reference policy, $\rho_{\mathrm{ref}} \leftarrow \rho_\phi$, which is later used to form log-ratio statistics and importance weights. For efficiency, token log-probabilities computed during SFT can be cached and reused in RKTO whenever the same (x, y_{pref}) pairs reappear.

RKTO Phase. For each preference batch $\{(x_i, y_{\mathrm{pref}}^{(i)}, m_{\mathrm{ref}}^{(i)})\}_{i=1}^{B}$: (i) compute normalized statistics $\hat{s}_\phi^{(i)}$ and $\hat{\eta}_0$ (Eq. (6)); (ii) evaluate R_{eff} (Eq. (4)) and R_{reflect} (Eq. (5)); (iii) form importance coefficients $c_i = w(\hat{s}_\phi^{(i)} - \hat{\eta}_0)$ and REINFORCE coefficients $d_i = c_i(1 - \alpha)(\mathrm{IoU}^{(i)} - b_{\mathrm{IoU}})$ with b_{IoU} the per-batch mean IoU baseline; and (iv) update parameters using the gradient estimator in Eq. (8). To maintain stability, we keep the RKTO learning rate smaller than the SFT learning rate (i.e., $\mathrm{LR}_{\mathrm{RKTO}} \ll \mathrm{LR}_{\mathrm{SFT}}$) and refresh ρ_{ref} on a fixed checkpoint schedule (or when validation plateaus).

Variance Reduction and Stability. We apply (a) clipping of importance weights to $[0, w_{\max}]$; (b) centering of rewards with per-batch baselines (including b_{IoU}); (c) gradient clipping; (d) optional averaging over multiple mask samples per input when decoding $\hat{m}$; and (e) smaller $\mathrm{LR}_{\mathrm{RKTO}}$ together with a conservative optimizer (e.g., AdamW with mild weight decay). Early stopping relies on validation metrics for instruction quality and reflection quality; the snapshot ρ_{ref} is advanced only when these metrics improve.

Algorithm 1. Iterative Training with SFT and RKTO

Require: Dataset $\mathcal{D}$, SFT epochs E_{SFT}, RKTO epochs E_{RKTO}
1: Initialize EVLM ρ_ϕ from Qwen2-VL-7B
2: **for** $e = 1$ to E_{SFT} **do**
3:     Minimize $\mathcal{L}_{\mathrm{SFT}}$ (Eq. 1); snapshot $\rho_{\mathrm{ref}} \leftarrow \rho_\phi$ periodically
4: **end for**
5: **for** $e = 1$ to E_{RKTO} **do**
6:     Sample batch $\{(x_i, y_{\mathrm{pref}}^{(i)}, m_{\mathrm{ref}}^{(i)})\}$
7:     Compute statistics (Eq. 6) and loss (Eq. 7)
8:     Update ϕ with estimator (Eq. 8); snapshot ρ_{ref} on schedule
9: **end for**

3.6   Monotonic Alignment Guarantee (Statement)

We measure joint alignment to human preferences via the composite divergence

$$\mathcal{K}(\phi) = \mathrm{KL}\big(\rho_\phi(y \mid x) \,\|\, \rho_{\mathrm{pref}}(y \mid x)\big) + \lambda_{\mathrm{ref}}\, \mathrm{KL}\big(\rho_\phi(r_{\mathrm{refl}} \mid x) \,\|\, \rho_{\mathrm{pref}}(r_{\mathrm{refl}} \mid x)\big), \quad (9)$$

where ρ_{pref} is the empirical human-preferred distribution, and $\lambda_{\text{ref}} \geq 0$ balances outputs and reflections.

Assumptions. (A1) Rewards are bounded: $R_{\text{eff}}, R_{\text{reflect}} \in [0, 1]$. (A2) The importance function $w(\cdot)$ is bounded and non-decreasing, applied to the log-ratio statistic s_ϕ with baseline η_0 (Eq. (3)). (A3) Learning steps are sufficiently small so that first-order Taylor approximations of the objectives are accurate. (A4) $\rho_\phi(\cdot \mid x)$ and $\rho_{\text{pref}}(\cdot \mid x)$ are mutually absolutely continuous on their support (standard for KL analysis).

Rationale. For fixed x, the gradient of each KL term has the standard log-derivative form, e.g.

$$\nabla_\phi \text{KL}\big(\rho_\phi(\cdot \mid x) \,\|\, \rho_{\text{pref}}(\cdot \mid x)\big) = \mathbb{E}_{y \sim \rho_\phi}\Big[\nabla_\phi \log \rho_\phi(y \mid x) \ \underbrace{\log \frac{\rho_\phi(y|x)}{\rho_{\text{pref}}(y|x)}}_{\text{log-density ratio}}\Big],$$

and analogously for the reflection term. The RKTO estimator (Eq. (8)) uses $c_i = w(\hat{s}_\phi^{(i)} - \hat{\eta}_0)$, where $\hat{s}_\phi^{(i)}$ is a sample log-density ratio and $w(\cdot)$ preserves its ordering. Multiplying by bounded rewards $R_{\text{eff}}, R_{\text{reflect}}$ reweights these ratios without flipping their signs. Consequently, the expected negative RKTO gradient points in a descent direction for $\mathcal{K}(\phi)$.

Guarantee. Under Assumptions (A1)–(A4), any parameter update that decreases the expected RKTO objective, $\mathbb{E}_x[\mathcal{L}_{\text{RKTO}}]$, also decreases the expected composite divergence, $\mathbb{E}_x[\mathcal{K}(\phi)]$. Thus, optimizing Eq. (2) improves alignment of both instructions and reflections with the human-preferred distributions.

4   Experiments

4.1   Model Architecture

Our model builds on the Qwen2-VL-7B architecture [49], which combines a 675M-parameter vision encoder with a 7.6B-parameter language model to strengthen multimodal reasoning. Naive Dynamic Resolution [8] allows variable-size visual inputs by dynamically tokenizing images without absolute position embeddings. We further incorporate 2D-RoPE and Multimodal Rotary Position Embedding (M-RoPE) [49] to encode spatial and temporal relations across text, images, and video, enabling precise positional reasoning.

4.2   Evaluation on REFLECTIVE-EDIT

Since generating editing instructions can be subjective, we evaluate EVLM with two complementary criteria on a fixed, stratified split of $N = 3{,}000$ unseen examples from REFLECTIVE-EDIT (balanced across edit types: color, style, texture, object replacement, and layout change).

Table 1. Accuracy comparison across different evaluators on the REFLECTIVE-EDIT benchmark. The last column shows the average accuracy across all evaluators.

Model	Gemini Pro 1.5	LLAMA 405B	GPT-4o	Claude 3.5 Sonnet	Human Evaluators	Avg. Accuracy
mPLUG-Owl [56]	44.8	45.1	43.3	42.7	49.0	44.8
mPLUG-Owl2 [57]	50.2	51.6	51.3	49.5	51.2	50.8
LLAVA [26]	48.3	46.8	47.2	45.9	43.5	46.3
MiniGPT-4 [64]	43.7	44.1	42.5	45.3	47.6	44.6
CogVLM [50]	41.4	42.2	40.7	39.6	55.2	43.8
InstructBLIP [7]	47.6	46.9	48.4	47.2	56.3	49.2
Qwen-VL [1]	49.3	50.4	48.6	47.8	52.4	49.7
LLAMA-3.2-11B [10]	55.5	57.2	56.3	54.8	60.1	56.7
LLAMA-3.2-90B [10]	64.7	63.5	66.1	64.3	58.9	63.5
EVLM-RKTO	**95.4**	**94.8**	**96.2**	**95.1**	**94.1**	**95.1**

1. **Human-labeled evaluation.** Annotators view the original image/video, the reference(s) (text/image/video, if present), and the candidate instruction side-by-side and assign a binary label YES/NO indicating whether applying the instruction would produce the intended edit. Ambiguities are resolved by majority vote among 3 raters; we retain per-rater labels for inter-rater statistics (Cohen's/Fleiss' κ).
2. **LLM-based evaluation.** We use four large language models as automated judges—Gemini Pro 1.5, LLaMA 405B, GPT-4o, and Claude 3.5 Sonnet— each returning YES/NO for the same 3,000 examples.

Evaluator Prompt (LLMs). We standardize the judge prompt across models:

You are given: (1) the original image (and reference image/text if present), (2) a human reference editing instruction, and (3) an automatically generated editing instruction. Your task: answer YES if the generated instruction semantically matches the human reference (i.e., would produce a visually similar edit to the target), otherwise answer NO. Consider object identity, target region, and transformation details. Do not hallucinate details beyond the provided inputs. Reply with a single token: YES or NO.

Annotator Guidance (Humans). Raters are instructed to: (i) compare original, reference(s), and candidate instruction; (ii) answer YES/NO to "Does this instruction, when applied, match the intended edit?"; (iii) rely on object semantics (e.g., "bag", "jacket"), region specificity (e.g., "left sleeve"), and transformation type (e.g., "change color", "add pattern"); (iv) avoid assuming context beyond shown reference(s); and (v) use majority vote for ambiguous cases. We report percent agreement and Cohen's κ between LLM judgments and the majority human label.

Table 2. Representative bootstrap statistics for the 3,000-example evaluation split. The 95% confidence intervals (CIs) are computed from 10,000 bootstrap resamples.

Evaluator	Mean Accuracy (%)	95% Bootstrap CI (%)
Gemini Pro 1.5	95.4	[94.2, 96.4]
LLaMA 405B	94.8	[93.5, 95.9]
GPT-4o	96.2	[95.1, 97.3]
Claude 3.5 Sonnet	95.1	[93.9, 96.2]
Human (majority)	94.1	[92.8, 95.4]
Average (EVLM-RKTO)	**95.1**	**[94.0, 96.0]**

Metrics and Statistics. For each evaluator (human and LLM), *Accuracy (%)* is the fraction of YES on the N examples. We compute 95% bootstrap confidence intervals (CIs) by drawing 10,000 resamples of size N with replacement and taking the 2.5^{th}–97.5^{th} percentiles of the accuracy distribution. Inter-rater agreement among human annotators is reported via pairwise Cohen's κ (and Fleiss' κ when > 2 raters).

Results. As reported in Table 1, EVLM-RKTO outperforms all baselines, with average accuracy **95.1%**. Representative bootstrap CIs for evaluators are shown in Table 2.

4.3   Implementation Details

We train EVLM in two phases. **SFT** optimizes Eq. 1 on Qwen2-VL-7B with AdamW (learning rate 5×10^{-5}), batch size $B = 64$ (with gradient accumulation if needed), and periodic snapshots of the reference policy $\rho_{\text{ref}} \leftarrow \rho_\phi$. **RKTO** then optimizes Eq. 2 with AdamW (learning rate 2×10^{-5}), using importance weights $w(s) = \text{clip}(\text{softplus}(s), 0, w_{\text{max}})$ with $w_{\text{max}} = 10$ and $\text{softplus}(s) = \log(1+e^s)$ (softplus threshold $\tau = 0.1$), three Monte-Carlo samples per example, per-batch

Table 3. Cross-benchmark performance (%) on multimodal reasoning and visual question answering benchmarks. Bold entries denote the best performance per row.

Benchmark	LLAMA-11B	Qwen2-7B	LLAVA-1.6	EVLM (RKTO)
MMMU (val, CoT)	50.7	**54.1**	35.8	53.0
MMMU-Pro (Vision)	33.0	43.5	–	**43.8**
MathVista (testmini)	51.5	58.2	34.6	**59.1**
ChartQA (test, CoT)	**83.4**	83.0	–	82.8
AI2 Diagram (test)	**91.1**	83.0	–	83.0
DocVQA (test)	88.4	**94.5**	–	93.1
VQAv2 (test)	75.2	–	**81.8**	77.4

reward baselines (including b_{IoU}), and gradient clipping. Unless otherwise stated, alignment hyperparameters are $\lambda_{\mathrm{ref}} = 0.2$, $\beta = (0.5, 0.2, 0.3)$, and $\gamma = 0.2$. We cache SFT teacher-forced log-probabilities to accelerate computation of s_ϕ and η_0 and reuse ρ_{ref} snapshots throughout RKTO. When parameter-efficient finetuning is used, we apply LoRA (rank 64, $\alpha = 16$, dropout 0.05) to language and cross-modal projection layers. Experiments run on 8×A100 (80 GB); SFT over 30K samples takes $\sim$48 GPU-hours and the RKTO stage $\sim$36 GPU-hours.

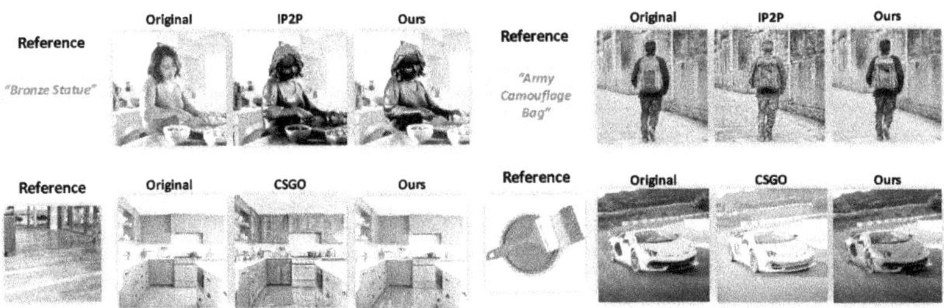

Fig. 4. Image Editing Results Using Reference Images or Text Prompts. The first row demonstrates EVLM's ability to refine vague textual prompts into precise editing instructions and to produce masks for targeted edits. The second row compares EVLM to an image-based editing baseline, illustrating improved alignment to reference-guided transformations.

4.4   General Visual Understanding

This section assesses EVLM's ability to retain generalization across multimodal benchmarks. As summarized in Table 3, EVLM achieves strong performance despite having fewer parameters than LLAMA-11B. It attains the highest scores on MathVista (59.1) and MMMU-Pro Vision (43.8), while matching or surpassing LLAMA-11B on DocVQA (93.1) and VQAv2. These results confirm that reflection-aware training enhances alignment and reasoning quality without compromising generalization.

4.5   Cross-Dimensional Visual Editing

EVLM serves as a plug-and-play module that refines textual prompts and identifies target objects for diffusion-based editors. When integrated with IP2P [3], it outperforms both text-only (IP2P) and image-based (CSGO) approaches in precision and controllability (Fig. 4). For video editing, we apply the Tune-A-Video recipe [53], where EVLM improves temporal consistency compared with Any-V2V [23].

For 3D editing, we employ 3D Gaussian Splatting [22] for scene reconstruction and compare against IN2N [14] and IG2G on the IN2N and 3DEgo datasets. In

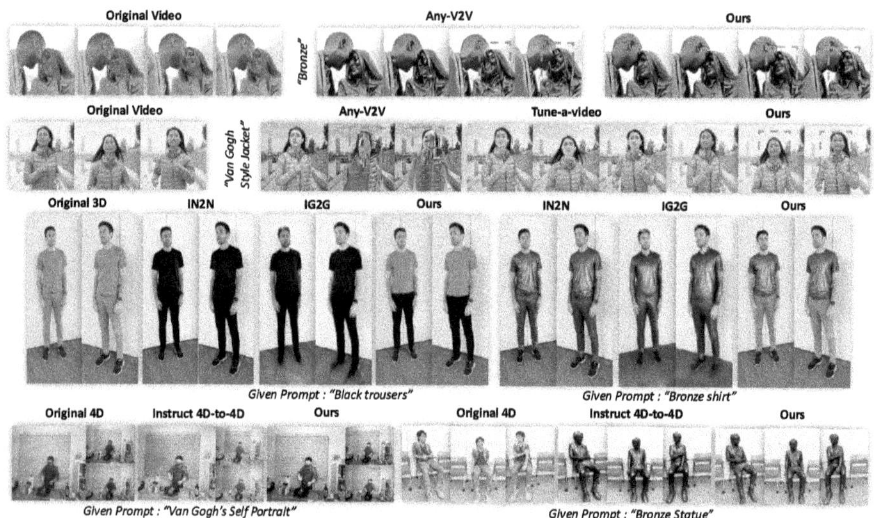

Fig. 5. Text-based editing across video, 3D, and 4D tasks. EVLM + IP2P surpasses baselines including Any-V2V, Tune-A-Video, IN2N, and IG2G. It delivers improved style consistency ("Bronze," "Van Gogh Style") and stable transformations across frames.

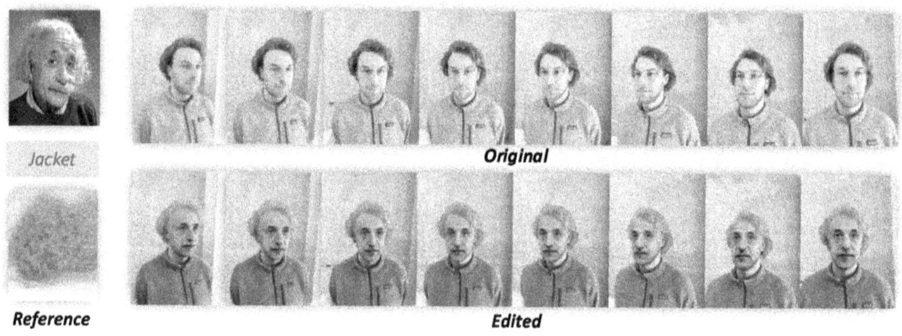

Fig. 6. Reference Image and Text. Examples of 3D editing results generated using EVLM + IP2P. The model produces context-aware editing instructions based on the reference content, autonomously interpreting the editing rationale to generate optimal instructions for the desired outcome. This example demonstrates multi-attribute editing, where the jacket is transformed into green, and the face is altered to resemble Einstein. (Color figure online)

4D editing, we evaluate on DyCheck, HyperNeRF, and DyNeRF/N3DV datasets using the frameworks of [33,52]. Across these tasks (Fig. 5), EVLM-guided edits exhibit superior spatial consistency, color coherence, and adherence to user intent. For 3D editing, we employ the standard Gaussian Splatting technique [22]. Figure 6 showcases a 3D editing example where the input to EVLM consists

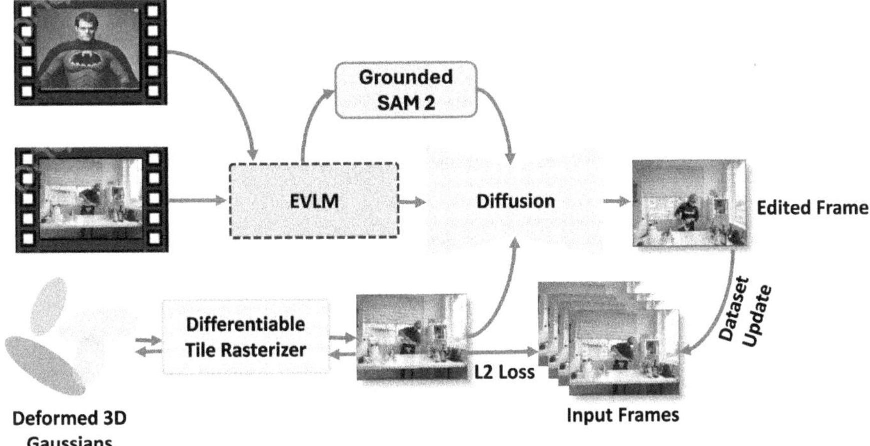

Fig. 7. The 4D editing pipeline guided by EVLM, which outputs both the editing instruction and the target object to be modified. The identified target object is passed through Grounded SAM 2 to generate precise masks, which guide local editing in the diffusion model based on the provided instruction. The edited frames are then iteratively updated in the dataset to ensure temporal and spatial consistency, while an L2 loss is applied between input and edited frames for quality refinement, resulting in a consistent and temporally smooth 4D dataset.

of four components: two images (Einstein and green threads), one text prompt (jacket), and multiple frames of a person's face. The model autonomously interprets the editing intent and generates the instruction: *Turn his face into Einstein and turn his jacket into green.* This instruction can then be utilized with [3] to perform the desired edits, as illustrated in the Fig. 6. The Fig. 7 demonstrates how EVLM processes the reference video and original video to generate context-aware editing instructions and execute the desired transformations. In this specific 4D editing example, the goal is to change the person's clothing into a Batman costume while preserving the face, as the reference video does not depict a Batman face. EVLM interprets the required editing from the reference and original videos, outputs the object label (clothing), and passes it to Grounded-SAM, which generates precise masks for the targeted region. These masks ensure that only the clothing is affected during the editing process. The editing instruction is then fed into a diffusion model, which applies the required transformation to the clothing while maintaining the integrity of other visual attributes, such as the face. The edited frames are iteratively replaced in the original dataset, creating a modified dataset aligned with the desired edits. Training is continued on this edited dataset to refine the alignment of deformed 3D Gaussians with the edited frames, ensuring the model's enhanced capacity to generalize and align with complex transformations.

4.6   Ablation Studies

We analyze the sensitivity of EVLM to key hyperparameters and design choices. Unless stated otherwise, *Accuracy (%)* denotes human-evaluated correctness of the final instruction, *Reflection Q* is a normalized human rating of reflection quality in $[0, 1]$, and IoU measures mask alignment with references.

RL Train-Set Size. We vary the number of RL (RKTO) training examples and observe consistent gains with more data (Table 4). Even with 5K examples, EVLM-RKTO significantly surpasses the base QWEN-2.5-VL-7B and EVLM-KTO, indicating that reflection within RL improves robustness and data efficiency.

Table 4. Performance of EVLM-RKTO under varying RL train-set sizes.

Model/Components	Size	Acc. (%)
Qwen-2.5-VL-7B	–	52.4
EVLM-KTO	5K	56.1
EVLM-RKTO	5K	59.1
EVLM-RKTO	7K	65.7
EVLM-RKTO	15K	78.2
EVLM-RKTO	30K	**94.1**

Reflection Weight λ_{ref}. The coefficient λ_{ref} controls the contribution of the reflection reward relative to the instruction-effectiveness term in the RKTO objective. As shown in Table 5, increasing λ_{ref} consistently improves both the reflection-quality score (*Refl. Q*) and the spatial alignment metric (IoU), indicating that a stronger reflection signal encourages more coherent reasoning and more consistent mask generation. However, when λ_{ref} becomes too

Table 5. Ablation on λ_{ref}. Higher weights strengthen reflection but can reduce fidelity.

λ_{ref}	Acc.	Refl. Q	IoU
0.00	88.0	0.62	0.41
0.05	90.5	0.68	0.46
0.10	92.3	0.72	0.51
0.20	**94.1**	0.78	0.58
0.50	93.4	0.80	0.56

large (e.g., 0.5), the model begins to overemphasize reflective segments at the expense of direct instruction fidelity, leading to a slight drop in overall accuracy (from 94.1% to 93.4%). This suggests that moderate reflection weighting ($\lambda_{\text{ref}} \approx 0.2$) achieves the best balance: the model reasons deeply enough to self-correct and justify edits while still maintaining concise, instruction-focused outputs. The results confirm that reflection is a beneficial regularizer when tuned appropriately but can dominate the optimization if overweighted.

Importance-Weight Cap w_{max}. The parameter w_{max} limits the magnitude of the softplus-transformed importance weights in the RKTO objective, acting as a form of gradient clipping for the ratio-based weighting term. As shown in Table 6, smaller caps make the opti-

Table 6. Ablation on w_{max}.

w_{max}	Acc.	Comment
5	92.1	conservative weighting
10	**94.1**	default, stable
20	93.6	slightly higher variance

mization more conservative—reducing gradient variance but also slowing convergence—whereas large caps accelerate training but risk unstable updates when outlier samples receive disproportionately high weights. The best trade-off occurs at $w_{\max} = 10$, which yields the highest overall accuracy (94.1%) with stable variance across runs. This indicates that moderate capping provides enough flexibility for the model to learn from confident preference samples while preventing occasional high-ratio terms from dominating the optimization.

Monte-Carlo Samples per Example. The number of Monte-Carlo (MC) samples determines how many stochastic rollouts are used to estimate the expectation in the importance-weighted gradient. Table 7 shows that increasing the number of samples steadily improves accuracy, as the gradient estimate becomes less noisy. However, gains saturate beyond three samples, while runtime grows linearly (roughly 1.6× cost for three samples and nearly 4× for eight). Thus, three samples offer the most practical balance between performance and efficiency—achieving the same 94.1% accuracy as heavier configurations but at half the computational expense.

Table 7. Ablation on MC samples for importance-weight estimation.

MC samples	Acc.	Runtime×
1	92.8	1.0
2	93.9	1.3
3	**94.1**	1.6 (default)
4	94.2	2.0
8	94.3	3.8

Reflection Reward Formulation. The reflection reward can be optimized either through a differentiable surrogate (providing smooth gradients) or with REINFORCE, which directly optimizes non-differentiable terms like IoU but introduces high variance. Table 8 highlights that using the surrogate alone produces stable but slightly under-optimized reflections, while REINFORCE alone yields noisy and less consistent learning. Combining both—using the differentiable surrogate for reflective reasoning and REINFORCE for the discrete IoU mask reward—achieves the best overall accuracy (94.1%), confirming that the hybrid formulation effectively balances stability and expressiveness in optimizing multimodal reflection signals.

Table 8. Surrogate vs. REINFORCE for reflection reward.

Method	Acc.	Note
Surrogate-only	93.8	lower variance
Surrogate + REINFORCE	**94.1**	best overall
REINFORCE-only	92.9	unstable

Effectiveness of Reflection-Aware RL Components. Ablating either reward term (R_{eff} or R_{reflect}) significantly lowers performance: removing the instruction-effectiveness term reduces accuracy from 94.1% to 89.2%, while removing the reflection reward drops it to 85.3%. This demonstrates that the two components are complementary—R_{eff} enforces semantic and spatial fidelity, while R_{reflect} shapes reasoning quality—and that both are required to achieve robust multimodal alignment.

Comparison with Alternative Training Objectives. To further isolate the contribution of reflection-aware optimization, we compare standard SFT, conventional KTO, and our RKTO variant, including two-step thinking versions where the model generates multiple reflective segments before output. As summarized in Table 9, EVLM-RKTO far surpasses all alternatives, achieving 94.1% accuracy compared to 75.1% for KTO and 67.2% for SFT. The results confirm that integrating explicit reflection rewards within preference-based reinforcement learning substantially improves both reasoning coherence and instruction accuracy.

Table 9. Training-objective comparison (human evaluation).

Method	Acc. (%)
EVLM-KTO	75.1
EVLM-KTO (2-step)	76.3
EVLM-SFT	67.2
EVLM-SFT (2-step)	65.1
Ours (EVLM-RKTO)	**94.1**

5   User Study

We evaluated contextual alignment via a user study with 50 participants (ages 20–40). Each participant was presented with pairs of references (text, image, or video) and the corresponding edited outputs across four editing types: 2D image editing, video editing, 3D editing, and 4D temporal editing. Participants rated contextual alignment on a 1–5 Likert scale, where 1 indicates poor alignment and 5 indicates perfect alignment. The study comprised 200 total edits (50 per type), with each participant evaluating 20 randomly sampled examples. Table 10 summarizes the mean alignment scores across all users.

Table 10. Contextual alignment from user study (1–5 scale). Higher is better.

Editing Type	EVLM	Best Baseline
2D Editing	**4.82**	IP2P: 4.32
Video Editing	**4.77**	Tune-A-Video: 4.41
3D Editing	**4.65**	IN2N: 4.38
4D Editing	**4.58**	Instruct 4D-to-4D: 4.42

6   Limitations

While EVLM significantly advances context-aware multimodal editing instruction generation, several limitations remain. The model's performance is closely tied to the quality and diversity of the REFLECTIVE-EDIT dataset; despite comprising 30K samples, it may not capture the full spectrum of complex or rare editing scenarios, limiting generalization to unseen tasks. Its reliance on human-rated rationales introduces subjectivity and potential bias into reflective reasoning and reward estimation. The reflection-aware fine-tuning (RKTO) stage also incurs higher computational cost than standard SFT, which constrains scalability and real-time applicability. In addition, EVLM may underperform when reference cues are ambiguous or conflicting (e.g., inconsistent text–image instructions) and remains primarily effective for localized, object-centric edits rather than large-scale scene transformations. The overall editing precision depends on the quality of mask generation (e.g., from Grounded-SAM), and errors in segmentation can propagate to final results. Finally, the current framework is limited to text–vision modalities and lacks mechanisms for continual or adaptive retraining that could enable faster adaptation to new styles, domains, or user preferences. Future work will explore scalable reflective optimization, richer multimodal inputs (including audio and temporal signals), and improved efficiency for real-time and interactive editing pipelines.

7   Conclusion

We present EVLM, a reflection-enabled vision–language model that resolves ambiguity in multimodal editing by combining Chain-of-Thought supervision with Reflection-aware KL-Divergence Target Optimization (RKTO). Trained on a curated REFLECTIVE-EDIT corpus of 30,000 CoT examples and validated on 3,000 held-out cases, EVLM produces concise, disambiguated editing instructions and target masks that improve downstream diffusion- and NeRF-based editors. Empirically, RKTO improves both instruction fidelity and reflection quality, yielding strong gains across image, video, 3D, and 4D editing tasks.

Future work will (i) expand CoT diversity to capture broader user styles and edge cases, (ii) formalize R_{reflect} with additional human-in-the-loop metrics (e.g., brevity vs. usefulness trade-offs), and (iii) study statistical significance and robustness under noisy references. We believe EVLM's reasoning-with-reflection paradigm generalizes beyond editing to other multimodal tasks that require interpretable decisions and subjective preference alignment.

A   Appendix

A.1   Dataset Details and Prompts

To train EVLM for multimodal editing instruction generation, we developed a comprehensive dataset that emphasizes diversity in input modalities and output clarity. The dataset preparation process involved **generation, augmentation**, and **refinement with human evaluation**, ensuring both the quality and breadth of data. In our training, we also include nearly 20% training samples from cross-domain datasets used in [5,6,54] in addition to our MME data. Cross-benchmark evaluations in the main paper use:

- MMMU/MMMU-Pro [59]
- MathVista [27]
- ChartQA [30]
- AI2 Diagram [21]
- DocVQA [31]
- VQAv2 [41]

Dataset Overview. The dataset consists of 30,000 samples distributed across six categories of input combinations, as shown in Table 11. Each sample contains:

- **Reference Input** (R): A combination of image, video, or text to provide editing context.
- **Original Input** (O): The target image or video requiring modifications.
- **Reflective Rationale and Instruction**: A detailed rationale generated by GPT-4o, followed by a human-reviewed editing instruction.

Generation of Paired Images. To prepare a subset where both the reference and the original are images, we generate paired image samples using DALL-E 3. Since we want EVLM to understand the relationship between the given reference and original visual cues, instead of relying solely on textual descriptions, we create **diptychs**, where the original input image and the edited output image are displayed side by side. This approach enhances alignment and correspondence between input-output image pairs by ensuring both visual and semantic consistency.

Table 11. Data Distribution for EVLM CoT Fine-Tuning

Reference	Original	# of Samples
Image	Image	10,000
Image+Text	Image	5,000
Video	Image	4,000
Image	Video	3,000
Video+Text	Image	3,000
Text	-	5,000

We use prompts designed to capture various transformations while maintaining the visual integrity of the input image. For instance, to generate the paired image from DALL-E 3 shown in Fig. 8, we use a prompt like:

Generate a diptych with two side-by-side images. On the left side, there should be a person standing confidently with a neutral expression, wearing casual clothing. On the right side, show the same person with a mustache while keeping the rest of the visual attributes unchanged.

Fig. 8. An example of a diptych generated for the EVLM dataset using DALL-E-3. The left panel displays the original image, while the right panel showcases the edited image, reflecting the instruction to add a mustache.

This methodology allows for generating a variety of image pairs that focus on specific edits, such as adding or removing objects, changing facial features, or modifying global attributes like color or style. By leveraging DALL-E 3's generative capabilities, we ensure that the resulting diptychs are coherent and contextually aligned, providing a strong foundation for fine-tuning EVLM.

Figure 8 illustrates an example of such a diptych. The left panel represents the reference image, while the right panel reflects the transformation specified by the prompt. This technique is particularly effective when working with samples where textual input is minimal or absent, as it allows EVLM to focus on interpreting visual relationships directly. We have furnished some examples in Table 12 where we use two reference images.

Overall, the diptych approach not only simplifies the editing process but also improves the model's understanding of contextual relationships between the original and modified visual content. By avoiding dependency on detailed textual descriptions, this method provides a streamlined and efficient pathway for multimodal image editing.

Table 12. Examples of Reference Images and Corresponding Editing Instructions

Reference Image 1	Reference Image 2	Editing Instruction
Einstein's face	Green threads	Turn his face into Einstein and turn his jacket green
Batman's face	Blue shirt	Turn his face into Batman and turn his shirt blue
Spider-Man's mask	Leather jacket	Turn his face into Spider-Man's mask and turn his jacket into leather
Mona Lisa's face	Green dress	Turn her face into Mona Lisa's face and turn her dress green
Robotic face	Black boots	Turn his face into a robotic face and turn his boots black
Cat's face	Yellow scarf	Turn their face into a cat's face and turn their scarf yellow
Superman's face	Red trousers	Turn his face into Superman's face and turn his trousers red
A clown's face	Striped T-shirt	Turn his face into a clown's face and turn his T-shirt into a striped pattern
Iron Man's mask	Metallic armor	Turn his face into Iron Man's mask and turn his outfit into metallic armor
A Viking's face	Fur coat	Turn his face into a Viking's face and turn his coat into fur
A painter's face	Multi-colored apron	Turn her face into a painter's face and turn her apron multi-colored
Santa Claus's face	Red and white suit	Turn his face into Santa Claus and turn his outfit into a red and white suit
A robot's head	Silver gloves	Turn his face into a robot's head and turn his gloves silver
A pirate's face	Black hat	Turn his face into a pirate's face and add a black hat
A magician's face	White gloves	Turn his face into a magician's face and turn his gloves white
A superhero's face	Cape	Turn his face into a superhero's face and add a red cape
A lion's face	Golden mane	Turn their face into a lion's face and turn their hairstyle into a golden mane
A wizard's face	Magic staff	Turn his face into a wizard's face and add a magic staff to his hand
A medieval knight's face	Shiny armor	Turn his face into a medieval knight's face and turn his outfit into shiny armor

In addition to using DALL-E 3 for generating paired images, we further leverage Stable Diffusion XL to create a diverse set of high-quality image samples. These generated images undergo pre-processing to ensure compatibility and are combined with other open-source datasets such as IN2N, 3DEgo, DyNeRF, and MSCOCO [25] to form reference-original pairs. This combination enriches

Table 13. Examples of Ambiguous Text and Image as References for Editing Instructions

Reference 1 (Text)	Reference 2 (Image)	Editing Instruction
Make it heroic	Superman's costume	Turn his outfit into Superman's costume while keeping his face unchanged
Give it a metallic vibe	A shiny silver texture	Turn the jacket into a silver metallic style while preserving the rest of the image
Bring a touch of royalty	A golden crown	Add a golden crown to the person's head without altering their facial features
Add an artistic feel	Van Gogh's painting	Turn his jacket into a style resembling Van Gogh's Starry Night painting
Transform into a character	Spider-Man's suit	Change his outfit into Spider-Man's suit while leaving his face intact
Make it winter-ready	A fur coat	Replace his jacket with a warm fur coat suitable for winter
Add a festive spirit	Christmas decorations	Turn her dress into a Christmas-themed outfit with red and white patterns
Create a futuristic look	A robotic arm design	Replace his arms with robotic prosthetics while keeping the rest of the image unaltered
Make it classic	A vintage tuxedo	Turn his outfit into a vintage tuxedo, keeping his hairstyle and face the same
Turn it into nature	A green leafy texture	Change her jacket into a pattern resembling green leaves
Add a magical touch	A wizard's robe	Transform his outfit into a wizard's robe with stars and moons
Show some adventure	A pirate's hat	Add a pirate's hat and an eyepatch while leaving the outfit unchanged
Brighten it up	A vibrant yellow scarf	Add a yellow scarf to her outfit without altering any other details
Make it sporty	A football jersey	Replace his shirt with a football jersey representing a famous team
Bring a cultural touch	A traditional Japanese kimono	Turn her outfit into a traditional Japanese kimono

the dataset with varied visual transformations and styles, enhancing the robustness of EVLM. For video-based pairs, we employ generative video models like CogVideoX-5B [55] and Stable Video Diffusion [2] to synthesize reference videos, while the original videos are sourced from publicly available datasets, including Kinetics [20] and Charades [43]. This multi-source, multi-modality data preparation process ensures that the training data encapsulates a wide range of visual edits and transformations, providing EVLM with the capability to generalize across diverse scenarios.

Reference Text. Figure ?? illustrates the distribution of instruction (Reference Text) lengths given as an input to EVLM. 8000/30000 samples have the reference text in addition to reference image or a video. EVLM's instructions, typically ranging from 1–4 words, demonstrate the model's ability to perform complex editing tasks with minimal and concise textual input, unlike InstructPix2Pix, which relies on more detailed instructions exceeding 4 words. Figure 9 provides a detailed view of the types of edits and their frequency, showcasing the dataset's balanced coverage of diverse editing tasks. We additionally created samples incorporating both textual and visual references, as illustrated in Table 13.

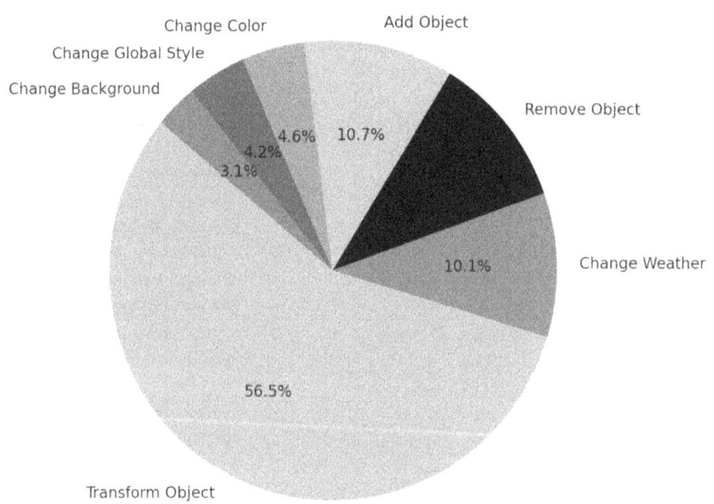

Fig. 9. Distribution of Edit Types in the EVLM Dataset. The dataset covers diverse editing tasks, with the majority focusing on object transformations.

Data Quality Assessment. To ensure high data quality, the dataset underwent the following refinements:

- **Human Evaluation**: Human raters validated and refined GPT-4o-generated rationales and instructions to align with subjective editing preferences.
- **Instruction Clarity**: Editing instructions were enriched to include sufficient detail, distinguishing them from the vague instructions typically used in baseline models.

– **Balanced Task Representation**: The dataset was carefully curated to balance global edits (e.g., changing weather or background) and local edits (e.g., object transformation or removal), as illustrated in Fig. 9.

Edit Diversity. The dataset spans a wide range of editing tasks, encompassing both global and local transformations. As shown in Fig. 9, the majority of tasks involve object transformations (56.5%), followed by weather changes (10.1%), object removals (10.9%), and object additions (10.7%). The diversity of edit types ensures that EVLM can generalize across varied scenarios.

By integrating reflective reasoning, human evaluation, and diverse multimodal inputs, this dataset provides a robust foundation for training EVLM to generate accurate and human-aligned editing instructions.

References

1. Bai, J., et al.: Qwen-vl: a versatile vision-language model for understanding, localization, text reading, and beyond. arXiv preprint arXiv:2308.12966 **1**(2), 3 (2023)
2. Blattmann, A., et al.: Stable video diffusion: scaling latent video diffusion models to large datasets. arXiv preprint arXiv:2311.15127 (2023)
3. Brooks, T., Holynski, A., Efros, A.A.: Instructpix2pix: learning to follow image editing instructions. In: Proceedings of the IEEE/CVF Conference on Computer Vision and Pattern Recognition, pp. 18392–18402 (2023)
4. Chen, X., Lin, M., Schärli, N., Zhou, D.: Teaching large language models to self-debug. In: The Twelfth International Conference on Learning Representations (2024). https://openreview.net/forum?id=KuPixIqPiq
5. Chen, Z., et al.: Internvl: scaling up vision foundation models and aligning for generic visual-linguistic tasks. In: Proceedings of the IEEE/CVF Conference on Computer Vision and Pattern Recognition, pp. 24185–24198 (2024)
6. Cheng, K., Li, Y., Xu, F., Zhang, J., Zhou, H., Liu, Y.: Vision-language models can self-improve reasoning via reflection. arXiv preprint arXiv:2411.00855 (2024)
7. Dai, W., et al.: Instructblip: towards general-purpose vision-language models with instruction tuning (2023)
8. Dehghani, M., et al.: Patch n'pack: Navit, a vision transformer for any aspect ratio and resolution. Adv. Neural Inf. Process. Syst. **36** (2024)
9. Dong, J., Wang, Y.X.: Vica-nerf: view-consistency-aware 3D editing of neural radiance fields. Adv. Neural Inf. Process. Syst. **36** (2024)
10. Dubey, A., et al.: The llama 3 herd of models. arXiv preprint arXiv:2407.21783 (2024)
11. Ethayarajh, K., Xu, W., Muennighoff, N., Jurafsky, D., Kiela, D.: Kto: model alignment as prospect theoretic optimization. arXiv preprint arXiv:2402.01306 (2024)
12. Ge, Y., Zhao, S., Li, C., Ge, Y., Shan, Y.: Seed-data-edit technical report: a hybrid dataset for instructional image editing. arXiv preprint arXiv:2405.04007 (2024)
13. Haque, A., Tancik, M., Efros, A., Holynski, A., Kanazawa, A.: Instruct-nerf2nerf: editing 3D scenes with instructions. In: Proceedings of the IEEE/CVF International Conference on Computer Vision (2023)
14. Haque, A., Tancik, M., Efros, A.A., Holynski, A., Kanazawa, A.: Instruct-nerf2nerf: editing 3D scenes with instructions. In: Proceedings of the IEEE/CVF International Conference on Computer Vision, pp. 19740–19750 (2023)

15. Hertz, A., Mokady, R., Tenenbaum, J., Aberman, K., Pritch, Y., Cohen-Or, D.: Prompt-to-prompt image editing with cross attention control. arXiv preprint arXiv:2208.01626 (2022)
16. Ho, J., et al.: Imagen video: high definition video generation with diffusion models. arXiv preprint arXiv:2210.02303 (2022)
17. Huang, J., et al.: Large language models cannot self-correct reasoning yet. arXiv preprint arXiv:2310.01798 (2023)
18. Kamata, H., Sakuma, Y., Hayakawa, A., Ishii, M., Narihira, T.: Instruct 3D-to-3D: text instruction guided 3D-to-3D conversion. arXiv preprint arXiv:2303.15780 (2023)
19. Kawar, B., et al.: Imagic: text-based real image editing with diffusion models. In: Proceedings of the IEEE/CVF Conference on Computer Vision and Pattern Recognition, pp. 6007–6017 (2023)
20. Kay, W., et al.: The kinetics human action video dataset. arXiv preprint arXiv:1705.06950 (2017)
21. Kembhavi, A., Salvato, M., Kolve, E., Seo, M., Hajishirzi, H., Farhadi, A.: A diagram is worth a dozen images. In: Leibe, B., Matas, J., Sebe, N., Welling, M. (eds.) ECCV 2016. LNCS, vol. 9908, pp. 235–251. Springer, Cham (2016). https://doi.org/10.1007/978-3-319-46493-0_15
22. Kerbl, B., Kopanas, G., Leimkühler, T., Drettakis, G.: 3D gaussian splatting for real-time radiance field rendering. ACM Trans. Graph. (ToG) **42**(4), 1–14 (2023)
23. Ku, M., Wei, C., Ren, W., Yang, H., Chen, W.: Anyv2v: a plug-and-play framework for any video-to-video editing tasks. arXiv preprint arXiv:2403.14468 (2024)
24. Li, Y., Yang, C., Ettinger, A.: When hindsight is not 20/20: testing limits on reflective thinking in large language models. In: Findings of the Association for Computational Linguistics: NAACL 2024. Association for Computational Linguistics (2024). https://aclanthology.org/2024.findings-naacl.237
25. Lin, T.-Y., et al.: Microsoft COCO: common objects in context. In: Fleet, D., Pajdla, T., Schiele, B., Tuytelaars, T. (eds.) ECCV 2014. LNCS, vol. 8693, pp. 740–755. Springer, Cham (2014). https://doi.org/10.1007/978-3-319-10602-1_48
26. Liu, H., Li, C., Wu, Q., Lee, Y.J.: Visual instruction tuning. Adv. Neural Inf. Process. Syst. **36** (2024)
27. Lu, P., et al.: Mathvista: evaluating mathematical reasoning of foundation models in visual contexts. arXiv preprint arXiv:2310.02255 (2023)
28. Lu, P., et al.: Learn to explain: multimodal reasoning via thought chains for science question answering. Adv. Neural. Inf. Process. Syst. **35**, 2507–2521 (2022)
29. Madaan, A., et al.: Self-refine: iterative refinement with self-feedback. Adv. Neural Inf. Process. Syst. **36** (2024)
30. Masry, A., Long, D.X., Tan, J.Q., Joty, S., Hoque, E.: Chartqa: a benchmark for question answering about charts with visual and logical reasoning. arXiv preprint arXiv:2203.10244 (2022)
31. Mathew, M., Karatzas, D., Jawahar, C.: Docvqa: a dataset for VQA on document images. In: Proceedings of the IEEE/CVF Winter Conference on Applications of Computer Vision, pp. 2200–2209 (2021)
32. Meng, C., Song, Y., Song, J., Wu, J., Zhu, J.Y., Ermon, S.: Sdedit: image synthesis and editing with stochastic differential equations. arXiv preprint arXiv:2108.01073 (2021)
33. Mou, L., Chen, J.K., Wang, Y.X.: Instruct 4D-to-4D: editing 4D scenes as pseudo-3D scenes using 2D diffusion. In: Proceedings of the IEEE/CVF Conference on Computer Vision and Pattern Recognition, pp. 20176–20185 (2024)

34. Ouali, Y., Bulat, A., Martinez, B., Tzimiropoulos, G.: Clip-dpo: vision-language models as a source of preference for fixing hallucinations in lvlms. arXiv preprint arXiv:2408.10433 (2024)

35. Pang, R.Y., Yuan, W., Cho, K., He, H., Sukhbaatar, S., Weston, J.: Iterative reasoning preference optimization. arXiv preprint arXiv:2404.19733 (2024)

36. Ramesh, A., et al.: Zero-shot text-to-image generation. In: ICML, pp. 8821–8831. PMLR (2021)

37. Rombach, R., Blattmann, A., Lorenz, D., Esser, P., Ommer, B.: High-resolution image synthesis with latent diffusion models. In: CVPR, pp. 10684–10695 (2022)

38. Ruiz, N., Li, Y., Jampani, V., Pritch, Y., Rubinstein, M., Aberman, K.: Dreambooth: fine tuning text-to-image diffusion models for subject-driven generation. In: Proceedings of the IEEE/CVF Conference on Computer Vision and Pattern Recognition, pp. 22500–22510 (2023)

39. Schulman, J., Wolski, F., Dhariwal, P., Radford, A., Klimov, O.: Proximal policy optimization algorithms. arXiv preprint arXiv:1707.06347 (2017)

40. Shao, R., et al.: Control4d: dynamic portrait editing by learning 4D GAN from 2D diffusion-based editor. arXiv preprint arXiv:2305.20082 (2023)

41. Shen, E., Singh, S., Kumar, B.: Generative visual question answering. arXiv preprint arXiv:2307.10405 (2023)

42. Shinn, N., Cassano, F., Gopinath, A., Narasimhan, K., Yao, S.: Reflexion: language agents with verbal reinforcement learning. In: Oh, A., Naumann, T., Globerson, A., Saenko, K., Hardt, M., Levine, S. (eds.) Advances in Neural Information Processing Systems, vol. 36, pp. 8634–8652. Curran Associates, Inc. (2023). https://proceedings.neurips.cc/paper_files/paper/2023/file/1b44b878bb782e6954cd888628510e90-Paper-Conference.pdf

43. Sigurdsson, G.A., Gupta, A., Schmid, C., Farhadi, A., Alahari, K.: Charadesego: a large-scale dataset of paired third and first person videos. arXiv preprint arXiv:1804.09626 (2018)

44. Singer, U., et al.: Make-a-video: text-to-video generation without text-video data. In: The Eleventh International Conference on Learning Representations (2023). https://openreview.net/forum?id=nJfylDvgzlq

45. Sun, Z., et al.: Aligning large multimodal models with factually augmented RLHF. arXiv preprint arXiv:2309.14525 (2023)

46. Sun, Z., et al.: Easy-to-hard generalization: scalable alignment beyond human supervision. arXiv preprint arXiv:2403.09472 (2024)

47. Tumanyan, N., Geyer, M., Bagon, S., Dekel, T.: Plug-and-play diffusion features for text-driven image-to-image translation. arXiv preprint arXiv:2211.12572 (2022)

48. Wang, K., Pan, J., Shi, W., Lu, Z., Zhan, M., Li, H.: Measuring multimodal mathematical reasoning with math-vision dataset. arXiv preprint arXiv:2402.14804 (2024)

49. Wang, P., et al.: Qwen2-vl: enhancing vision-language model's perception of the world at any resolution. arXiv preprint arXiv:2409.12191 (2024)

50. Wang, W., et al.: Cogvlm: visual expert for pretrained language models (2023)

51. Weng, Y., et al.: Large language models are better reasoners with self-verification. In: The 2023 Conference on Empirical Methods in Natural Language Processing (2023). https://openreview.net/forum?id=s4xIeYimGQ

52. Wu, G., et al.: 4D gaussian splatting for real-time dynamic scene rendering. In: Proceedings of the IEEE/CVF Conference on Computer Vision and Pattern Recognition, pp. 20310–20320 (2024)

53. Wu, J.Z., et al.: Tune-a-video: one-shot tuning of image diffusion models for text-to-video generation. In: Proceedings of the IEEE/CVF International Conference on Computer Vision, pp. 7623–7633 (2023)
54. Xu, G., Jin, P., Hao, L., Song, Y., Sun, L., Yuan, L.: Llava-o1: let vision language models reason step-by-step. arXiv preprint arXiv:2411.10440 (2024)
55. Yang, Z., et al.: Cogvideox: text-to-video diffusion models with an expert transformer. arXiv preprint arXiv:2408.06072 (2024)
56. Ye, Q., et al.: mPLUG-Owl: modularization empowers large language models with multimodality. arXiv preprint arXiv:2304.14178 (2023)
57. Ye, Q., et al.: mPLUG-Owi2: revolutionizing multi-modal large language model with modality collaboration. In: 2024 IEEE/CVF Conference on Computer Vision and Pattern Recognition (CVPR), pp. 13040–13051. IEEE (2024)
58. Yu, T., et al.: RLAIF-V: aligning mllms through open-source ai feedback for super gpt-4v trustworthiness. arXiv preprint arXiv:2405.17220 (2024)
59. Yue, X., et al.: Mmmu: a massive multi-discipline multimodal understanding and reasoning benchmark for expert AGI. In: Proceedings of the IEEE/CVF Conference on Computer Vision and Pattern Recognition, pp. 9556–9567 (2024)
60. Zhang, L., et al.: Tinychart: efficient chart understanding with visual token merging and program-of-thoughts learning. arXiv preprint arXiv:2404.16635 (2024)
61. Zhang, L., Agrawala, M.: Adding conditional control to text-to-image diffusion models. arXiv preprint arXiv:2302.05543 (2023)
62. Zhao, H., et al.: Ultraedit: instruction-based fine-grained image editing at scale. arXiv preprint arXiv:2407.05282 (2024)
63. Zhou, D., Wang, W., Yan, H., Lv, W., Zhu, Y., Feng, J.: Magicvideo: efficient video generation with latent diffusion models. arXiv preprint arXiv:2211.11018 (2022)
64. Zhu, D., Chen, J., Shen, X., Li, X., Elhoseiny, M.: Minigpt-4: enhancing vision-language understanding with advanced large language models. arXiv preprint arXiv:2304.10592 (2023)
65. Zhuang, J., Wang, C., Lin, L., Liu, L., Li, G.: Dreameditor: text-driven 3D scene editing with neural fields. In: SIGGRAPH Asia 2023 Conference Papers, pp. 1–10 (2023)

Geometry-Aware Energy-Based Image Modelling

Zoe Wu[(✉)]

Harvard University, Cambridge, UK
`zoewu@college.harvard.edu`

Abstract. Recent advances in image generative models have enabled rich collaborations between humans and AI systems. Among these, Energy-Based Models (EBMs) learn an energy landscape that guides noised samples toward high-probability regions. Unlike diffusion models that use fixed time schedules, EBMs possess equilibrium properties that enable user feedback during generation without destabilizing the distribution. However, current EBM research primarily optimizes for high-fidelity images, offering little control over the trade-off between semantic realism and fine-grained diversity—an essential feature for interactive creative applications. Artists and creatives thus lack a modality to balance semantic coherence (e.g., "a red apple") with creative variation (e.g., apples of different shapes or colors). To address this, we introduce a geometry-aware annealing framework for EBMs. We propose a directionally-aware annealing variable that leverages local geometric information to directionally adjust the effective noise level during sampling. Such an annealing feedback mechanism that allows users to explore higher-diversity sample contenders before selectively generating realistic images from chosen contenders. Together, these techniques enable a controllable balance between fidelity and creativity, advancing the use of EBMs for interactive creative AI.

1   Introduction

Recent advances in generative modeling have transformed how humans interact with AI systems in creative domains such as art, design, and storytelling (Heigl 2025; Gozalo-Brizuela and Garrido-Merchán 2023). Image generative models in particular have made it possible for artists to co-create with AI, yet most current systems still treat users as static prompt providers (Ko et al. 2023) rather than dynamic collaborators who influence the generation process. A central challenge in interactive creative AI is enabling models to respond meaningfully to user feedback during generation—adapting to evolving creative intent while maintaining coherence and quality in the produced artifacts.

Diffusion models (Ho, Jain, and Abbeel 2020; Dhariwal and Nichol 2021; Rombach et al. 2022) have become the dominant paradigm for high-fidelity image generation, forming the foundation of systems such as DALL·E and Stable Diffusion. They achieve remarkable sample quality through a gradual denoising

© The Author(s), under exclusive license to Springer Nature Switzerland AG 2026
K. Woodward et al. (Eds.): CLIP 2026, CCIS 2865, pp. 133–145, 2026.
https://doi.org/10.1007/978-3-032-16893-1_9

process that learns a score function over multiple time steps. However, this design introduces two key limitations for interactive creative use. First, the long sampling trajectories (Salimans and Ho 2022) that ensure high fidelity also constrain real-time interaction—users cannot easily modify or steer the generation process mid-sampling. Second, diffusion models rely on fixed, pre-defined time schedules; altering these schedules in response to user feedback can destabilize the sampling dynamics and degrade quality (Lin et al. 2024).

Energy-Based Models (EBMs) (Yilun and Mordatch 2020) offer a promising alternative for real-time, interactive generation. Like diffusion models, EBMs are grounded in statistical mechanics, but they differ fundamentally in their treatment of system dynamics. Diffusion models model non-equilibrium trajectories that evolve toward data distributions, whereas EBMs define equilibrium distributions directly through an energy function (Yu and Huang 2025). This equilibrium property enables EBMs to incorporate user feedback continuously—adaptations to the generated image can be made without restarting the entire sampling process. Such responsiveness makes EBMs particularly suitable for creative settings where users wish to explore, refine, and iterate fluidly with an AI system.

A core dimension of interactive creative control is managing the fidelitydiversity tradeoff. High-fidelity samples adhere closely to learned distributions, producing semantically realistic outputs (e.g., a correctly rendered red apple). High-diversity samples, by contrast, deviate from dominant modes to explore more varied or unconventional outcomes (e.g., apples of different colors, shapes, or contexts) (Naeem et al. 2020). This tradeoff (Fig. 1) parallels the classic explorationexploitation balance in machine learning: models that exploit low-energy modes yield coherent but repetitive samples, while those that explore more broadly foster novelty but risk incoherence. For creative applications, the ability to modulate this tradeoff interactively–shifting from realism toward imaginative variation–is essential.

Traditional approaches control this balance by scaling the step size (Fig. 2) during sampling: increasing noise promotes diversity, while reducing it increases

Fig. 1. Left: high fidelity samples exhibit low distributional difference from training samples. Right: high diversity samples exhibit more unlikely configurations but may present different adaptations of the prompt.

fidelity. However, isotropic noise scaling treats all directions in image space equally, indiscriminately perturbing both critical and peripheral features. This uniform variance can degrade important structural details even when only subtle semantic variations are desired. To address this, we propose incorporating directionally-aware geometric information into the sampling dynamics.

Specifically, we introduce a Riemannian metric tensor (Girolami and Calderhead 2011; Do Carmo and Flaherty Francis 1992) that captures the local curvature of the energy landscape, enabling directionally-tuned noise adaptation in EBMs. This tensor encodes spatially and semantically dependent covariances between pixels, allowing the model to adjust perturbations based on local geometry. For instance, in the apple example, our method can preserve the structural integrity of the stem while selectively varying the color and texture of the fruit.

Building on this foundation, we propose an interactive annealing framework that allows users to dynamically control the balance between fidelity and diversity during generation. EBMs enable compositional generation – unlike diffusion models which must start from noise, users can input to EBMs previous samples. Users can thus use the annealing variable to begin with high-diversity explorations and progressively refine chosen samples toward semantically faithful outputs, or conversely, inject creative variation into realistic images.

Our experiments demonstrate that this geometry-aware adaptive annealing scheme provides fine-grained user control over the fidelitydiversity spectrum without compromising sample quality. Together, these results suggest that equilibrium-based generative models equipped with Riemannian feedback mechanisms can form the basis of responsive, interactive AI systems that meaningfully participate in real-time creative workflows.

2   Background

Langevin Dynamics. Langevin dynamics, originating from statistical mechanics, form the foundation of modern generative frameworks such as diffusion and energy-based models (Song and Ermon 2019). The goal is to draw samples from a target distribution

$$p(\mathbf{x}) \propto \exp\left[-\mathcal{E}(\mathbf{x})\right],$$

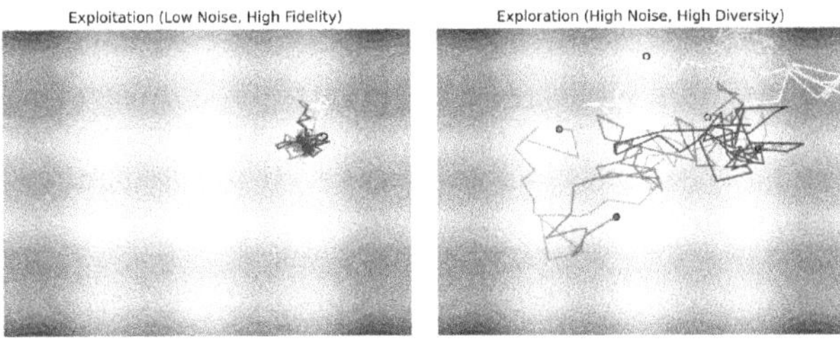

Fig. 2. Top: high exploitation of low energy (high probability) modes leads to high fidelity low diversity samples. Bottom: high exploration leads to higher mode coverage, yet may not converge to lowest energy.

where $\mathcal{E}(\mathbf{x})$ denotes the potential (energy) landscape that assigns low energy to high-probability regions.

Standard Langevin dynamics define a continuous-time stochastic differential equation (SDE):

$$d\mathbf{x}_t = -\tfrac{1}{2}\nabla_{\mathbf{x}}\mathcal{E}(\mathbf{x}_t)\,dt + d\mathbf{B}_t,$$

where $\mathbf{B}_t$ represents a D-dimensional Brownian motion. The drift term $-\tfrac{1}{2}\nabla_{\mathbf{x}}\mathcal{E}(\mathbf{x}_t)$ drives samples toward low-energy (high-probability) regions, while the stochastic term $d\mathbf{B}_t$ introduces exploration by injecting isotropic Gaussian noise.

In practice, directly integrating the continuous SDE is computationally intractable. Instead, a discrete-time approximation is used with step size $\lambda > 0$:

$$\mathbf{x}^{(k+1)} = \mathbf{x}^{(k)} - \tfrac{\lambda}{2}\nabla_{\mathbf{x}}\mathcal{E}(\mathbf{x}^{(k)}) + \boldsymbol{\omega}^{(k)}, \quad \boldsymbol{\omega}^{(k)} \sim \mathcal{N}(\mathbf{0}, \lambda\mathbf{I}).$$

This stochastic iterative process alternates between energy-guided descent and noise-driven exploration, allowing sampling from complex multimodal distributions.

Energy-Based Models. Energy-Based Models (EBMs) define an unnormalized density over data as

$$p_{\boldsymbol{\theta}}(\mathbf{x}) = \frac{\exp[-\mathcal{E}_{\boldsymbol{\theta}}(\mathbf{x})]}{Z_{\boldsymbol{\theta}}},$$

where $\mathcal{E}_{\boldsymbol{\theta}}(\mathbf{x})$ is a learnable energy function parameterized by $\boldsymbol{\theta}$, and $Z_{\boldsymbol{\theta}}$ is the intractable partition function ensuring normalization.

The standard maximum-likelihood learning objective is given by

$$\mathcal{L}_{\mathrm{ML}}(\boldsymbol{\theta}) = \mathbb{E}_{\mathbf{x}\sim p_D}[-\log p_{\boldsymbol{\theta}}(\mathbf{x})],$$

where p_D denotes the empirical data distribution. The gradient of this loss can be expressed as

$$\nabla_{\boldsymbol{\theta}}\mathcal{L}_{\mathrm{ML}} \approx \mathbb{E}_{\mathbf{x}^{+}\sim p_D}\left[\nabla_{\boldsymbol{\theta}}\mathcal{E}_{\boldsymbol{\theta}}(\mathbf{x}^{+})\right] - \mathbb{E}_{\mathbf{x}^{-}\sim q_{\boldsymbol{\theta}}}\left[\nabla_{\boldsymbol{\theta}}\mathcal{E}_{\boldsymbol{\theta}}(\mathbf{x}^{-})\right],$$

where $\mathbf{x}^{+}$ are positive samples from the data distribution and $\mathbf{x}^{-}$ are negative samples drawn from the model distribution $q_{\boldsymbol{\theta}}$, typically via Langevin dynamics.

Intuitively, this update decreases the energy of real data while increasing the energy of model-generated samples, progressively aligning the model distribution $q_{\boldsymbol{\theta}}$ with the true data distribution p_D. The interplay between energy minimization and stochastic exploration is crucial to the expressivity of EBMs, particularly in high-dimensional visual domains.

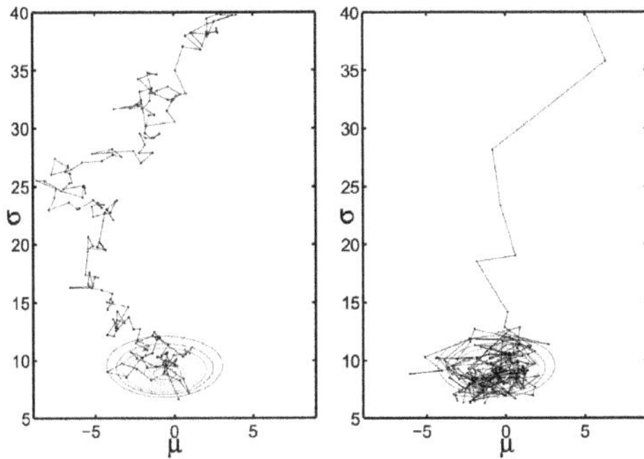

Fig. 3. Generating samples with Riemannian MALA (right) leads to faster convergence to target distribution than standard MALA (left) (Girolami and Calderhead 2011).

Riemannian Langevin and Manifold MALA. Standard Langevin dynamics assume a Euclidean geometry where exploration is isotropic, treating all directions equally. This assumption becomes inefficient when sampling from high-dimensional, curved probability manifolds such as image or latent spaces, where modes can be highly anisotropic. The *Manifold Metropolis-Adjusted Langevin Algorithm (Manifold MALA)* extends classical Langevin dynamics to Riemannian manifolds by adapting the sampling process to the local geometry of the target distribution. (Fig. 3)

Let $\mathbf{z} \in \mathbb{R}^d$ denote parameters defined on a Riemannian manifold $\mathcal{M}$ equipped with a metric tensor $\mathbf{G}(\mathbf{z})$. The metric tensor specifies local curvature, defining how distances and directions are measured. The Riemannian gradient of an energy function $\mathcal{E}(\mathbf{z})$ is given by

$$\nabla_{\mathbf{z}}^{(\mathrm{Rie})} \mathcal{E}(\mathbf{z}) = \mathbf{G}^{-1}(\mathbf{z}) \nabla_{\mathbf{z}}^{(\mathrm{Euc})} \mathcal{E}(\mathbf{z}),$$

where $\nabla_{\mathbf{z}}^{(\mathrm{Euc})}$ is the Euclidean gradient. Substituting this into Langevin dynamics yields the Riemannian update rule:

$$\mathbf{z}^{(k+1)} = \mathbf{z}^{(k)} - \tfrac{\lambda}{2}\, \mathbf{G}^{-1}(\mathbf{z}^{(k)}) \nabla_{\mathbf{z}} \mathcal{E}(\mathbf{z}^{(k)}) + \mathbf{G}^{-1}(\mathbf{z}^{(k)}) \boldsymbol{\omega}^{(k)}$$

This formulation introduces anisotropic exploration: motion is accelerated along flat directions of the energy landscape and slowed in steep regions, improving mode coverage and convergence.

Because discretization introduces bias, Manifold MALA employs a Metropolis-Hastings correction. At each step, a new candidate $\mathbf{z}^{\mathrm{new}}$ is sampled from a Riemannian-adjusted Gaussian proposal distribution centered at $\mathbf{z}^{(k)}$. The proposal is then accepted or rejected using the Metropolis ratio:

$$r = \min\left(1, \frac{p(\mathbf{z}^{\mathrm{new}})\, q(\mathbf{z}^{(k)}|\mathbf{z}^{\mathrm{new}})}{p(\mathbf{z}^{(k)})\, q(\mathbf{z}^{\mathrm{new}}|\mathbf{z}^{(k)})}\right),$$

where $q(\cdot|\cdot)$ denotes the local Gaussian proposal density incorporating $\mathbf{G}(\mathbf{z})$. This step ensures that the resulting Markov chain satisfies detailed balance and converges to the true target distribution.

3   Methods

We extend standard Langevin sampling by incorporating a Riemannian (Fisher-based) metric tensor into the dynamics:

$$\mathbf{x}^{(k+1)} = \mathbf{x}^{(k)} - \frac{\lambda}{2}\mathbf{G}^{-1}(\mathbf{x}^{(k)})\nabla_{\mathbf{x}}\mathcal{E}_\theta(\mathbf{x}^{(k)}) + \mathbf{G}^{-1/2}(\mathbf{x}^{(k)})\boldsymbol{\omega}^{(k)}$$

Fisher Information Matrix. For an Energy-Based Model $p_\theta(\mathbf{x}) \propto \exp[-\mathcal{E}_\theta(\mathbf{x})]$, the Riemannian (Fisher) metric on $\mathbf{x}$-space is defined as

$$\mathbf{G}_{\mathrm{FIM}}(\mathbf{x}) = \mathbb{E}_{\mathbf{x} \sim p_\theta}\left[\nabla_{\mathbf{x}}\log p_\theta(\mathbf{x})\nabla_{\mathbf{x}}\log p_\theta(\mathbf{x})^\top\right] \tag{1}$$

$$= \mathbb{E}_{\mathbf{x} \sim p_\theta}\left[\nabla_{\mathbf{x}}\mathcal{E}_\theta(\mathbf{x})\nabla_{\mathbf{x}}\mathcal{E}_\theta(\mathbf{x})^\top\right], \tag{2}$$

since $\nabla_{\mathbf{x}}\log p_\theta(\mathbf{x}) = -\nabla_{\mathbf{x}}\mathcal{E}_\theta(\mathbf{x})$. The expectation in (2) is intractable because p_θ is unnormalized and high-dimensional. We thus adopt a stochastic sample-based estimator.

Stein Score Metric Tensor. The Stein score metric tensor provides a smooth, data-dependent Riemannian structure over the energy landscape of an EBM. For a point $\mathbf{x} \in \mathbb{R}^D$, the metric is defined as

$$\mathbf{G}_\tau(\mathbf{x}) = \tau\, \mathbf{s}(\mathbf{x})\mathbf{s}(\mathbf{x})^\top + \mathbf{I},$$
$$\mathbf{s}(\mathbf{x}) = \nabla_{\mathbf{x}}\log p_\theta(\mathbf{x}) = -\nabla_{\mathbf{x}}\mathcal{E}_\theta(\mathbf{x}),$$

where $\mathbf{I}$ is the $D \times D$ identity matrix and $\tau > 0$ is a user-controlled coefficient that scales anisotropy in the score direction.

This formulation parallels the construction of rank-1 anisotropic metrics such as those in (Azeglio and Di Bernardo 2025; Pascanu and Bengio 2013) and provides a smooth mechanism to interpolate between exploration and fidelity by modulating the geometric influence of the score field.

The metric $\mathbf{G}_\tau(\mathbf{x})$ combines the isotropic Euclidean geometry with an additional curvature term that stretches the manifold along the gradient of the log-density. It has several desirable properties: (1) when $\tau = 0$, it reduces to the standard Euclidean metric; (2) increasing τ strengthens alignment with the score direction, concentrating movement along high-probability regions; (3) $\mathbf{G}_\tau(\mathbf{x})$ remains symmetric positive definite for all $\tau > 0$.

Sherman–Morrison Inverse. For $\mathbf{G}_\tau(\mathbf{x}) = \mathbf{I} + \tau\, \mathbf{s}\mathbf{s}^\top$, the Sherman–Morrison formula gives

$$\mathbf{G}_\tau^{-1} = \mathbf{I} - \frac{\tau\, \mathbf{s}\mathbf{s}^\top}{1 + \tau\|\mathbf{s}\|_2^2},$$
$$\mathbf{s}(\mathbf{x}) = \nabla_{\mathbf{x}}\log p_\theta(\mathbf{x}) = -\nabla_{\mathbf{x}}\mathcal{E}_\theta(\mathbf{x}),$$

The determinant is $\det(\mathbf{G}_\tau) = 1 + \tau\|\mathbf{s}\|_2^2$, and the inverse square root used for the noise term is

$$\mathbf{G}_\tau^{-1/2} = \mathbf{I} - \left(1 - \frac{1}{\sqrt{1 + \tau\|\mathbf{s}\|_2^2}}\right)\frac{\mathbf{s}\mathbf{s}^\top}{\|\mathbf{s}\|_2^2}. \tag{3}$$

Algorithm 1. Riemannian Langevin Sampling for EBMs

Initialize $\mathbf{x}$
for iteration $= 1$ to K **do**
    Compute $\mathbf{s} = \nabla_{\mathbf{x}}\mathcal{E}_\theta(\mathbf{x})$
    Compute metric $\mathbf{G}^{-1}$ and $\mathbf{G}^{-1/2}$ from $\mathbf{s}$
    Sample noise $\eta \sim \mathcal{N}(\mathbf{0}, \lambda\,\mathbf{G}^{-1})$
    Update:
$$\mathbf{x}^{\text{new}} = \mathbf{x} - \tfrac{\lambda}{2}\mathbf{G}^{-1}\mathbf{s} + \eta$$
    Accept or reject $\mathbf{x}^{\text{new}}$
end for
return samples $\{\mathbf{x}\}$

---

4   Results

4.1   Toy Experiment

Setup. We designed a toy example using a 3D Gaussian distribution $p(x, y, \theta)$. The conditional case fixes θ, corresponding to a 2D slice of the Gaussian. An energy-based model (EBM) was trained on both unconditional and conditional data, and performance was evaluated via the Wasserstein distance (WD) between generated and target samples. To study the trade-off between fidelity (closeness to the conditional slice) and diversity (coverage of the full Gaussian), we interpolated between unconditional and conditional energies, similar to varying the classifier-free guidance (CFG) weight in diffusion models.

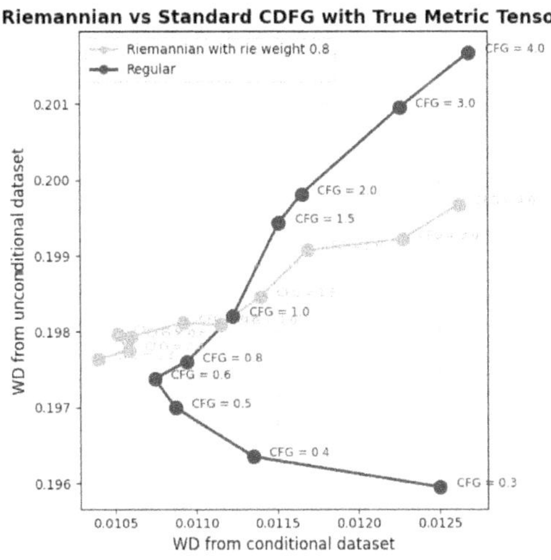

Fig. 4. Orange curves represent Riemannian generation (fixed $\tau = 0.5$), while Blue curves represent the Euclidean baseline. The x-axis measures adherence to the target distribution, and the y-axis measures adherence to the broader, unconditional distribution (lower is better for both). CFG weights represent conditional weight, with lower representing highly conditional samples.

Results. The results indicate that the Riemannian approach yields a more balanced and interpretable relationship between fidelity and diversity. In the Euclidean (standard) case, adjusting the conditional weight produces a nonlinear trade-off: improvements in faithfulness to the conditioning data come at a steep loss of sample diversity and hence faithfulness to unconditional data. This behavior reflects that the gradient updates are not aligned with the intrinsic structure of the data distributions.

By contrast, the Riemannian formulation introduces a geometry-aware metric $\mathbf{G}_\tau(\mathbf{x})$ that rescales updates according to the local geometry. This mechanism suppresses motion along directions where the conditional and unconditional distributions differ most, so variations in the conditional weight lead to smoother, more proportional changes in sample behavior. Overall, the Riemannian metric regularizes the evolution of fidelity and diversity, mitigating the geometric distortion that causes instability in standard conditional sampling. (Fig. 4, 5)

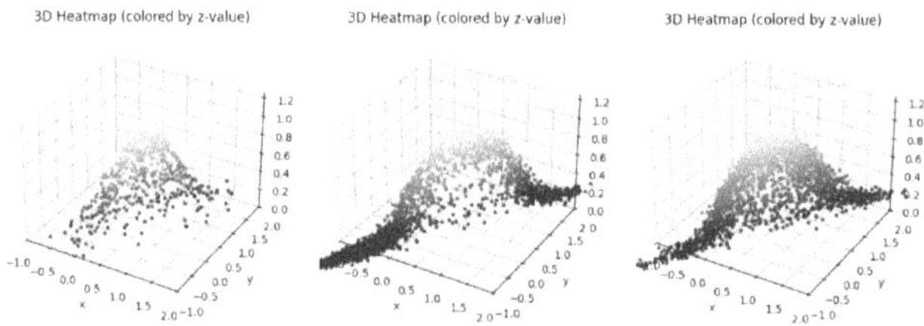

Fig. 5. In the Euclidean case, movement between the conditional and unconditional densities follows a nonlinear, curved path–analogous to the "C"-shaped trade-off curve. Under the Riemannian metric, the local geometry adapts to gradient structure, flattening the curvature of this path. This alignment allows the Riemannian sampler to interpolate linearly between conditional and unconditional distributions, producing the approximately straight (linearized) trade-off.

4.2   Image Dataset

Setup. We conduct experiments on the ImageNet dataset (Deng et al. 2009) to evaluate the behavior of our energy-based model (EBM) under both Euclidean and Riemannian parameterizations. ImageNet contains over one million high-resolution images across 1,000 object categories, serving as a standard benchmark for large-scale generative modeling and representation learning. Following the setup in (Yilun and Mordatch 2020), images are normalized to the $[0, 1]$ range and resized to 128×128 resolution. The EBM is trained directly on pixels using a ResNet-128 backbone, optimized via maximum likelihood estimation through short-run Langevin dynamics. This allows the model to learn an unnormalized energy function that captures both global image structure and local texture statistics.

To examine the effects of geometry and step size, we compare two sampling strategies: (1) scaling the step size term isotropically, as in standard EBMs, and (2) scaling it directionally using a Riemannian metric tensor $\mathbf{G}_\tau(\mathbf{x})$. The first approach controls diversity through a global scalar variance, while the second adapts the stochasticity to the local curvature of the energy landscape.

Qualitative Results. Qualitatively, isotropically scaling the step size increases variance but often degrades image quality (Fig. 6), yielding overly smooth or noisy, desaturated samples. In contrast, directionally scaling with the Riemannian tensor (Fig. 7) modulates updates along semantically aligned directions of the data manifold. As the Riemannian weight (τ) increases, the sampler better follows the intrinsic geometry of the energy landscape–enhancing structural and color fidelity even as diversity is maintained. This geometry-aware preconditioning thus provides a more effective mechanism for achieving high-quality, stable image generation without sacrificing controlled variability.

Fig. 6. Left: standard Euclidean EBM. Right: Riemannian EBM with $\tau = 0.5$. From top to bottom: smaller step sizes correspond to more muted, less structured images. The Riemannian metric (right) adaptively rescales gradient and noise directions based on local geometry of the energy landscape, allowing both structure and color, even for large step sizes.

Fig. 7. From top to bottom: increasing τ in Riemannian EBM increases the fidelity-diversity tradeoff, with samples exhibiting high color diversity despite minimal semantic differences. $\tau = 0$ corresponds to Euclidean EBMs.

4.3   Interactive Generation

User-Feedback Mechanism.ϕ We introduce a continuous feedback variable $\phi \in [0, 1]$ that controls the tradeoff between fidelity and diversity, where $\phi = 1$ emphasizes high fidelity (precise, mode-following samples) and $\phi = 0$ emphasizes high diversity (broad, exploratory samples). This variable jointly modulates two geometric hyperparameters in the Riemannian EBM: the step size λ and the Riemannian scaling weight τ. The parameters are defined as

$$\lambda(\phi) = \lambda_{\max} - \phi\,(\lambda_{\max} - \lambda_{\min}), \tag{4}$$

$$\tau(\phi) = \tau_{\min} + \phi\,(\tau_{\max} - \tau_{\min}), \tag{5}$$

with $\lambda_{\min} = 80$, $\lambda_{\max} = 200$, $\tau_{\min} = 1$, and $\tau_{\max} = 2$. Low ϕ values correspond to exploratory sampling with smaller step sizes and minimal geometric scaling, favoring diversity, whereas high ϕ values correspond to higher fidelity, with larger step sizes and stronger Riemannian alignment to the score field 8. This formulation ensures a consistent, continuous interpolation between exploration and precision through coordinated adjustment of both step magnitude and geometric anisotropy.

Fig. 8. From top to bottom: increasing ϕ in our interactive feedback mechanism generates higher-fidelity yet less diverse samples. Here, $\phi = 0$ corresponds to $\tau = 1.0, \lambda = 200$ and $\phi = 1$ corresponds to $\tau = 2.0, \lambda = 80$.

Interactive Sample Generation. The interactive refinement process enables user to generate an initial set of diverse samples under exploratory settings ($\phi = 0.0$, larger τ, and step size λ), encouraging broad variation and creative outcomes. Users can visually inspect these intermediate results and select those aligning with their creative intent. An example workflow would generate initial, diverse samples with a few Langevin steps as in Fig. 9, then selected samples are reintroduced into the Riemannian energy-based model 10 under higher-fidelity conditions ($\phi = 1.0$), where smaller step sizes and stronger geometric alignment guide the dynamics toward semantically coherent, high-quality refinements. This two-stage workflow—exploration followed by guided convergence—facilitates human-in-the-loop control over both diversity and precision in the generative process. The use of EBMs enable multi-step generation, while standard diffusion models enforce only time-based sampling, where initial samples may only be Gaussian noise.

5   Discussion

We have introduced a geometry-aware framework for energy-based image generation that leverages Riemannian metrics to modulate sampling dynamics according to local geometric structure. This approach provides a principled baseline for

Fig. 9. Samples from landscape classes generated with $\phi = 0.00$ ($\tau = 1.0$, $\lambda = 200$) for 50 Langevin steps. Users can intervene mid-sampling and select samples they want to refine for fidelity.

Fig. 10. Select samples from Fig. 9 reran through Riemannian EBM for increased fidelity $\phi = 1.0$ ($\tau = 2.0$, $\lambda = 80$) for 150 more Langevin steps.

equilibrium-based sampling, demonstrating that fidelitydiversity trade-offs can be controlled without relying on time-dependent diffusion schedules. By aligning the sampling process with the intrinsic curvature of the learned energy landscape, the proposed method regularizes trajectories and enables interpretable modulation between exploration and exploitation. Looking ahead, this work offers a foundation for future research on *Equilibrium Matching*–a paradigm in which generative processes evolve toward stable equilibrium distributions under learned geometric constraints. Such models could unify energy-based and diffusion perspectives, providing equilibrium-consistent pathways for controllable and physically grounded generation.

References

Azeglio, S., Di Bernardo, A.: What's Inside Your Diffusion Model? A Score-Based Riemannian Metric to Explore the Data Manifold (2025). arXiv preprint arXiv:2505.11128

Deng, J.; Dong, W.; Socher, R., Li, L.-J., Li, K., Fei-Fei, L.: Imagenet: A large-scale hierarchical image database. In: 2009 IEEE conference on computer vision and pattern recognition, pp. 248–255. IEEE (2009)

Dhariwal, P., Nichol, A.: Diffusion models beat gans on image synthesis. Adv. Neural. Inf. Process. Syst. **34**, 8780–8794 (2021)

Do Carmo, M.P., Flaherty Francis, J.: Riemannian geometry, vol. 2. Springer (1992)

Girolami, M., Calderhead, B.: Riemann manifold Langevin and Hamiltonian Monte Carlo methods. J. R. Stat. Soc. Ser. B Stat Methodol. **73**(2), 123–214 (2011)

Gozalo-Brizuela, R., Garrido-Merchán, E.C.: A survey of Generative AI Applications (2023). arXiv preprint arXiv:2306.02781

Heigl, R.: Generative artificial intelligence in creative contexts: a systematic review and future research agenda. Management Review Quarterly, pp. 1–38 (2025)

Ho, J., Jain, A., Abbeel, P.: Denoising diffusion probabilistic models. Adv. Neural. Inf. Process. Syst. **33**, 6840–6851 (2020)

Ko, H.-K., Park, G., Jeon, H., Jo, J., Kim, J., Seo, J.: Large-scale text-to-image generation models for visual artists' creative works. In: Proceedings of the 28th international conference on intelligent user interfaces, pp. 919–933 (2023)

Lin, S., Liu, B., Li, J., and Yang, X.: Common diffusion noise schedules and sample steps are flawed. In: Proceedings of the IEEE/CVF winter conference on applications of computer vision, pp. 5404–5411 (2024)

Naeem, M.F., Oh, S.J., Uh, Y., Choi, Y., Yoo, J.: Reliable fidelity and diversity metrics for generative models. In: International conference on machine learning, pp. 7176–7185. PMLR (2020)

Pascanu, R., Bengio, Y.: Revisiting natural gradient for deep networks (2013). arXiv preprint arXiv:1301.3584

Rombach, R., Blattmann, A., Lorenz, D., Esser, P., Ommer, B.: High-resolution image synthesis with latent diffusion models. In: Proceedings of the IEEE/CVF conference on computer vision and pattern recognition, pp. 10684–10695 (2022)

Salimans, T., Ho, J.: Progressive Distillation for Fast Sampling of Diffusion Models (2022). arXiv preprint arXiv:2202.00512

Song, Y., Ermon, S.: Generative modeling by estimating gradients of the data distribution. Adv. Neural Inf. Process. Sys. **32** (2019)

Yilun, D., Mordatch, I.: Implicit Generation and Generalization in Energy-Based Models (2020). arXiv preprint arXiv:1903.08689

Yu, Z., Huang, H.: Nonequilbrium physics of generative diffusion models. Phys. Rev. E **111**(1), 014111 (2025)

Author Index

© The Editor(s) (if applicable) and The Author(s), under exclusive license
to Springer Nature Switzerland AG 2026
K. Woodward et al. (Eds.): CLIP 2026, CCIS 2865, p. 147, 2026.
https://doi.org/10.1007/978-3-032-16893-1

GPSR Compliance
The European Union's (EU) General Product Safety Regulation (GPSR) is a set
of rules that requires consumer products to be safe and our obligations to
ensure this.

If you have any concerns about our products, you can contact us on

ProductSafety@springernature.com

In case Publisher is established outside the EU, the EU authorized
representative is:

Springer Nature Customer Service Center GmbH
Europaplatz 3
69115 Heidelberg, Germany

www.ingramcontent.com/pod-product-compliance
Ingram Content Group UK Ltd.
Pitfield, Milton Keynes, MK11 3LW, UK
UKHW020819080726
473059UK00007B/2338